Suck It Up, Cupcake

**Stop screwing yourself and
get the life you want**

Dennis A. McCurdy

Adam Beck Publishing
212 Main St.
Sturbridge, MA 01566

Copyright
Suck It Up, Cupcake © 2022 Dennis A. McCurdy

For more information,
email dennis@find-away.com
ISBN 978-0-9798863-2-4

Dedication

As always, I dedicate this book to my two wonderful adult children Rebecca (Becky) McCurdy, and Adam McCurdy and grandchildren now and the ones on the way. And to all those who helped me along the way and are too numerous to mention.

Appreciation

Readers/editors/early helpers
In alphabetical Order
Justin Bellinger Becky Bruso Sharon Como
Charlie Cook Mike Fafford
Janet Hall
Steve Hall
Alix McNitt
Rebecca McCurdy Douglas Senecal, aka Doug
Danger
Maria Senecal
Rita Schiano

Illustrations

Patrick Carlson, cartoonist/Illustrator
https://www.patrickcarlson.net/

Foreword

Have you ever said to yourself, "I should be doing better in life? Why is it that everyone else always seems to get all the lucky breaks, but I never do? Why is it that I try so hard and never seem to get ahead?" When I met Dennis McCurdy in 2010, I was asking myself those same questions.

When we met in his insurance office in Sturbridge, MA that day, I said, "I don't understand why I'm not financially secure? Not rich? I'm Doug Danger, the *Guinness Book of World Record*s holder for long-range motorcycle jumping. Plus, I own a bar. I should be rich, right? Instead, I'm broke. I feel like I'm lost, with no direction in life. And I'm getting too old to keep risking my life jumping motorcycles. Sure, living this bar, lifestyle is fun, but I'm not getting ahead."

Dennis' response was very straightforward. "So, sell the bar, quit jumping, and suck it up cupcake!"

I was stunned and sure didn't expect to hear that. "So how am I supposed to make money?"

"Look, Doug, you have an incredible story to tell. A story the world must hear. You're a Stage 4 cancer survivor; you broke numerous world records. You lived through a bike crash that put you in a coma for a month and you had to relearn everything…. how to walk…who you family was…*everything* all over again. and you're still going. Yet, you have nothing to show for it. Your *fortune* is in your story."

He suggested I join the local Toastmasters club, an international group that cultivates public speakers. Dennis was a very involved member. In fact, he started the local group. He explained it was a place where I could gain the confidence and improve my skills to speak in public.

"You beat everyone in the world jumping your bike. So, explain how you did it. A lot of people fail trying to achieve their goals in life, but there is a formula to success. You had to figure out the formula to jump a motorcycle over *forty-two cars*. And you succeeded in doing that. You know how to figure out a success formula"

Dennis saw something in me that I didn't see in myself. "I'll show you how," he offered. "But if you don't listen, don't learn, don't take action, you will fail."

I was all in!

Dennis explained how some of the things I was doing were sending me in the wrong direction, such as spending money on things that didn't make money, like the bar. These self-defeating behaviors were destroying any chance I had of making progress.

"Every business must have a plan and a formula to succeed," he said. "While plans may vary, the same rules for success apply. Actually, they apply to most everything in life."

When you look at a person as successful as Dennis, you start to understand he just might have the secret formula to make things happen.

He had me start writing speeches to tell my story. He mentored and encouraged me to include the business mistakes I had made and what I learned from them. Above all, Dennis held me accountable to myself and to my future. Dennis explained the finer details of a speaker's success, such as having a book. "A book provides people with inspiration to take home after a speech," he said. "When you are receiving $5,000 for a speech, you can easily double your money by selling 50-to-100 books at the back of the room after the speech."

I didn't know how to write or publish a book. Dennis gave me sound advice on how to develop habits that were productive. One of the most constructive ideas he suggested was to promise myself to write for a half hour every day; make it a commitment, an investment in my future. When I struggled to write, Dennis talked about finding a co-writer who could help me complete this endeavor. He suggested I look for someone who was "busy as heck; they always finish the things they start." I called my cousin Steve Hall (a very busy man) to do the writing with me, and I am proud to say, I now have a published book about my life: *Doug Danger Dare to Dream - From tragedy to triumph: A daredevil's ride.*

Today, I earn more money speaking than I ever did dragging my ramps halfway across the country, setting them up, and risking my life to jump over an insane number of automobiles, trucks, snakes, and even jumbo jets.

You've taken the first step to reach your goals by having this book in your hands. In these chapters, you will learn to develop new strategies to bring your thinking to a level that you had previously considered unimaginable.

Get ready to go on a journey to places you have always dreamed of going. Get ready for success, financial freedom, reaching new heights, and accomplishing things you never believed were possible.

Let Dennis' example of success become your steps to achieving your dreams. I followed his path, and now it's your turn. I hope your journey is as fun, fulfilling, and gratifying as mine has been. Remember, the harder you work, the luckier you will seem to get.

Happy landings! ~ Doug Danger

Introduction

The problem for many of us as I see it, is that there is too much hype, too much rah, rah information on living the ideal life. Often the hype's only true purpose is to make money for the information peddler. Too often these "influencers" ignore focusing on the basic principles developed over time that work.

There are tried-and-true methodologies and processes that do work, and which can move you towards the life you want; move you to better health and even more wealth, which is what we all need. I know this to be true because I have researched them and put them into practice.

Everything I learned, everything I know, and everything I will share with you in this book came from self-education. Truth be told, I barely made it out of high school, even failed English. But I am a sponge. I've always strived to learn from anyone about everything. And one of the things I discovered is that all you have to do is to ask. Most people will tell you what they know, and most are willing to help you. I guess you could say that I got my education on the learn-as-you-go plan.

And here's what that education brought forth in my life. I've started ten businesses, (I'm still working in 4 of them). I've owned 29 properties, built houses, rehab houses, bought and sold foreclosures, and owned a business that was designated a 5 Star agency. I've also written three books, over 200 blogs and articles, developed and conducted personal development workshops, and became a Firewalking instructor. And who knows what's next.

Introduction

Now, you might think: "I couldn't possibly do all that or even some of what he has accomplished." Well, you are wrong. So, Suck It Up, Cupcake and get started. Start by reading this book. Don't just leave it on the shelf collecting dust. Reading this book will help you avoid the cost of wasting away your time, your days, your nights, and getting you nowhere. Not to mention the cost of your unused talents and abilities or the cost of finding a unique ability and living more of the life you are meant to live.

All I ask of you is to be open to changing your beliefs and your thinking, and to start associating with the right people, people who will support you in your quest for a better life. All you have to do is to have the courage to try. Start by taking small steps, making slow changes. Have a plan. It's never too late.

The well-known business coach, Dan Sullivan, said something particularly inspiring. He said that at age 70 he was working on his 25-year plan. As I finish this book, I am now 72 and working on my 25-year plan. No matter what age you are or how many things you have done or have gone wrong, you need a plan. There will always be problems and struggles. For every level, there's another devil. But don't let that stop you. Just suck it up, cupcake and keep moving forward.

Within these pages you will find solutions, insights and processes that will help you to understand yourself and help you move forward. I am sharing with you the lessons I've learned over many years. I'll show you how to take actions that will change your life if you are willing to do the work.

I don't know how old you are or what your life circumstances may be, but I do know this: the longer you wait to read this book, the longer you wait to take action, the longer you wait to use the principles I'm laying out for you here, the less likely you are to get the life you want. So start reading this book today. Start making changes. Start moving toward the life that you want. No more excuses. Suck It Up, Cupcake and start.

Preface

I didn't write this book just for you. I also wrote it for myself, as a reminder to us both, you, and me that self-improvement is a process, a continual process. And speaking of continual processes, this book is an example of that.

My idea for *Suck It Up, Cupcak*e, took root many years ago. Okay, I'll be honest … many, *many* years ago. I thought about it, talked about, took volumes of notes, thought about and talked about it some more, and then about two years ago, I got serious about writing this book.

One important thing I learned during those years is that I am my own worst enemy, thanks to procrastination. Procrastination is my biggest obstacle, and one, I think, that is pretty much true for the majority of people. I would almost guarantee it. I was allowing fear and procrastination to sabotage me even though I knew my idea for this book was a good one.

So yes. I wrote this book for us. And I promise if you use even some of the ideas and tools presented, you will improve. I did, and that's why you are now holding this book in your hands. I sucked it up, tossed the cupcake to the side, started writing and kept going.

As Confucius said, "It does not matter how slow you go as long as you don't stop."

~ Dennis McCurdy

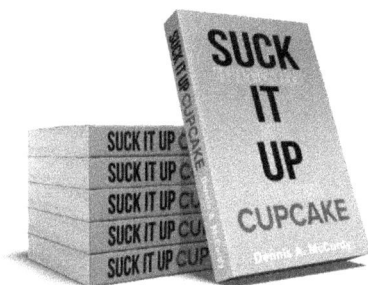

Want more success?

Get Your Free

10 tips for starting your own Mastermind Group?

Sign up Now!

Click the link and I'll send you a free PDF

https://lp.constantcontactpages.com/su/hsQ3KV2

Time to Suck It Up, Cupcake!

Suck It Up, Cupcake
Table of Contents

1

START

Every great dream begins with a dreamer.
Always remember, you have within you the
strength, the patience, and the passion to reach for
the stars to change the world.
~ Harriet Tubman

If you could do anything you wanted, what would it be? When I ask people this, they'll tell me, "I would like to have my own business," "I would like to lose weight, or "I could marry the person of my dreams," "Make more sales calls," "Start writing my book," "Do my art," or myriad of other things. So, then I ask, "Why don't you?" and here come the reasons, aka the excuses, and they are plentiful.

"I don't know what to do."

"I don't have the time."

"I just can't get myself started."

And then I say, "If you start to do it by this Friday, I will give you $10,000. Do you think you'd get it done?"

Or what if I said, "If you make those ten cold calls by Friday, lose eight pounds this month, or start your book, I will give you $10,000." What do you think the answer would be? The answer, of course, is "Yes!"

My point is this. You could do it if you wanted to, except you just don't want to. You are comfortable with the way you are, even if you say or think you aren't.

Most of us can do far more than we imagine. It's just a matter of putting it at the top of our list, making it a priority, pushing through the membrane of fear and complacency, and *actually working at it* a little every day. If you truly want to know what is important to you and your priorities, look at what you did today, yesterday, last week, last month, last year. You will find your true priorities and can identify which were not, even if you said they were.

One day while having lunch with a friend, he said he had not been accomplishing all the things he wanted. I asked what those things were, and he rattled off a list some short-term goals/objectives.

"Okay," I said. "Let's make a list of your goals." Once we had the list of doable goals completed, I told him, "Now you have to give me a check for $500. And if you don't finish the goals we agreed on in the next thirty days, I get to keep the five-hundred bucks."

His response? "Oh . . . I'm not ready for that yet."

The truth is, he may never be ready to achieve those things he said he wanted. And it wouldn't matter if the payoff was $500 or $5,000. If you are not mentally, emotionally, and intellectually ready—if you haven't *decided* to START, you won't.

So, here's my first bit of advice for you: Suck it up, cupcake, and START!

"The secret to getting ahead is just getting started."
~ Mark Twain

Isaac Newton's first law of motion, sometimes referred to as the law of inertia, states, "An object at rest stays at rest, and an object in motion stays in motion." That's all you need to do—be in motion toward your goals. Every small step counts especially small, consistent steps. One little action toward your goal each day adds up to 365 steps (accomplishments) in a year.

There is magic in action, and the universe rewards action. How? By providing opportunities. Opportunities are always presenting themselves to you. But what do you do? Do you choose to run toward opportunities or away from them? Beliefs and fears play a major factor in your decision to run away, or grab hold of the opportunity. I'll explain this in detail in chapters 2 and 3.

No watchers . . .

What do I mean by *no watchers*? People will call me about coming to a Firewalk, and they'll say, "Can I come to the Firewalk and watch?" A Firewalk is people walking across 1,000+ degree hot coals. The reason or lesson is that things we often think are impossible aren't once we learn the lesson—the how-to. The rest is getting out of our own way and pushing through the fear, taking that first step.

My reply to those people is always, "No, you can't. The Firewalk requires full participation. It is for people serious about facing their fears, overcoming challenges, and going deep within themselves."

Watchers are people who sit on the sidelines. They are not in the game, nor do they want to get in the game. They simply want to watch and judge. As has been said by many, "There are three types of people in the world; those who make things happen, those who watch things happen, and those who wonder, *what happened!*"

People who come to the Firewalk are on a journey of discovery and action. They *want* to make things happen. They are there for a *purpose*, to be *with doers*, to *participate* with the other people at the Firewalk who are on a similar journey of exploring, learning, and taking action.

So here is a question; which are you? A doer or watcher? If you are the latter and want to change, then Suck It Up, Cupcake and START. Do something, do anything no matter how small, towards your dream, your goal. You can change almost everything in your life. A little bit of effort will go a long way. It doesn't have to be a crazy, wild, and insane effort. Making small amounts of progress daily can lead to the big change. People often believe they have to go to extremes to implement and create change. Remember, little hinges swing big doors.

Here are classic examples: The crash diet, the extreme workout, and other fads are unsustainable and lead to one destiny: derailing the goal. Growth needs to be developed sustainably. You will read the word *sustainable* many times in this book because it's important to set up circumstances in your life that are easily and sustainable. The key is building habits through small, consistent changes and challenges that are sustainable over the long run. Just as *sustainability* applies to the environment, remember that *you* are the greatest influence on *your* environment.

Suppose you want to cut down on carbs. If you eliminate your usual two pieces of toast from breakfast, you might feel deprived. The new habit might not be sustainable because it's too drastic. However, if you start by cutting out a half piece of toast, then another a week or so later until you've weaned yourself off toast, success is more likely sustainable. You've eliminated that sense of deprivation.

The same approach can apply when you're eating out. Put as little as one-eighth initially in a to-go box before you start to eat. Sometimes I will get something like a donut or a scone and immediately throw half in the trash before I eat the whole thing. I've struck a deal with the staff at a restaurant I frequent to limit me to five home fries with breakfast.

The key is consistency; committing to the habits you build incrementally will lead to the bigger-picture results you seek. Reaching the goal takes time and patience. Be careful not to set yourself up for failure by:

- Not being *specific*; be clear about what you want
- Expecting perfection in the beginning, or expecting perfection, period
- Setting too short a time frame
- Making the goal too large (in the short run)

Falling into these traps can leave you discouraged and with decreased motivation.

My Toastmasters friend, Marty Evans, author of *300 Pounds and Running*, and the podcast by the same name, talks about the first time he stepped onto the treadmill weighing 360 pounds and his goal of running a marathon—26.2 miles. He lasted ten seconds. Undaunted, the second time, he lasted fourteen seconds. Marty viewed the extra four seconds as *progress*. He also realized it was only the start of the entire process, not the finish line. He knew not to confuse the beginning with the end results. And yes, Marty did complete a marathon.

I've been asked what the best book is to buy for personal development—for reaching one's goals and dreams. The answer is (ding, ding, ding) *Mine! The t*ruth is, there are many good books that will give you ideas, tips, suggestions, and techniques to help you. It does not matter which book you buy. (Okay, it matters to me.) The reality is nothing will happen if you buy a book and put it on the shelf. The book just becomes a "shelf help" book, whose sole purpose is dust collection. Action is always a key to moving forward.

To my point, a few years ago, I was helping a friend clean her garage. I found a set of workbooks and videotapes for a real estate course. Also in that box was the invoice—$1,590. But the books were unopened, the videos still sealed. That dream of buying real estate just sat on the garage floor like so many dreams.

Unfortunately, most people choose not to take action in their lives until their backs are against the wall. I am talking about everything from health to wealth. Why wait for a crisis to begin building more of the life you want? Don't be like the government or most people—waiting until things hit the fan, creating chaos and crisis. It can certainly be difficult to muster the courage to change. This is another good reason to start small and keep it sustainable.

Here is an important principle. Your brain doesn't like change, challenges, or anything that may create work or discomfort. It is a scientific fact; your brain likes homeostasis (balance), staying still, saving energy, and being safe. So, anything that looks like change or challenge, even for the better, causes us to pull back and be cautious. That is how humans have survived for so long. And since you are reading this book, I bet you would like to do more than survive. You want to thrive. And yes, you can!

We only improve and grow when we have had enough. When the pain we feel, the comfort of staying the same can no longer be tolerated, or it just pisses us off—that is when we make changes. This is kind of a twist on the expression, "No pain, no gain," in the sense that we need to feel the emotional pain to push us to the pain of doing what will help us gain.

Sure, I procrastinate, get lazy, let fear get in my way, and I suspect you do, too. We all do. It's called being human. So, don't worry. Today is a new day, and yesterday is over. Avoid worrying about the past or fearing the future. Focus on what you can do today, leading to progress on your journey because today is all you have. If you steer off track, do not be disheartened. Just find ways to get yourself back on track as soon as possible make a get-back-on-track plan. Lots more on that later.

Suck It Up, Cupcake and START. That does not mean you have to drop everything now and abandon your responsibilities. It *does* mean you take a good, hard look at yourself, where you are, and where you prefer or want to be. Do whatever it takes, assuming it is legal, and you are not injuring someone. Think big and start small.

Here are some suggestions:

- Take one action step, even if it is small. Now, repeat, repeat, repeat.
- Break tasks down into five-minute increments. Even spending only two minutes on something may be enough to get you started. You will be surprised at how well this works.
- Don't focus on losing twenty-five pounds; focus on eating only half of that cupcake or losing one pound or even ¼ of a pound.

Always remember no program, idea, or system works unless you put in the work; that's the bottom line.

Justin and Becky, have been waiting for the right time to start their side business.

Choose a goal. What small steps can you START? Write them here or do to www.dennismccurdy.com under free stuff and you find a goal setting worksheet:

_____

_____

_____

Jiminy Cricket, the famous little guy in Walt Disney's *Pinocchio,* used to sing:

> *When you wish upon a star.*
> *Makes no difference who you are.*
> *Anything your heart desires will come to you.*

Unfortunately, that's BS. How many times have you wished things were different? How often have you heard someone else wish their life was better or different? Or that they looked better, were healthier, earned more money?

You can't get things by wishing; you only get things by doing. Wishing is a victim mentality; doing is a victory mentality. Most of us don't suffer from a lack of ideas. We suffer from a lack of action. I often refer to this as the "intention/action gap," which is huge. Jim Rohn, an author and one of the best-known personal development workshop presenters in America, said, "Don't wish things were easier; wish you were better." To that, I would add, "Don't wish things were better or easier, just start now to be better."

What do you need to do to make things better? Don't wait. Take action now. Anytime you have an idea, follow it up with action. That action can be as small as writing the idea on paper and taping it to a wall, door, or refrigerator. Anywhere you will see it every day. The great Chinese philosopher Lao-Tzu said, "The journey of a thousand miles begins with one first step."

Next, create an action plan, a series of small, sustainable steps. Who is going to do what, when? Who is going to help you; who's going to kick you in the ass when you need it? Yes. Find somebody who will kick you in the ass, hold you accountable. Remember, too; it is about sustainability. Here is a quote I keep on my desk.

"Success seems to be largely a matter of hanging on after others have let go."
~ William Feather

Did you know that Coca-Cola sold only 400 bottles of soda the first year in business? Or that Shake Shack sprouted from a hot dog cart in Madison Square Park in Manhattan? We sometimes forget that everything starts small. It's a process. The ones who thrive are those who keep their heads down and keep moving forward. Yes, they do look up to see the direction they are traveling. That's what progress is about. Remember, Rome wasn't built in a day, but some part of it was. So, do your part today.

"You don't have to see the whole staircase, just take the first step."
~ Dr. Martin Luther King, Jr.

Interestingly, once we START, we begin to gain confidence. Confidence doesn't necessarily come first, which is what most people think. Usually, fear and doubt are first in line. As we move forward, confidence begins to build. But always—and I mean always—be aware of fear and doubt. They will always be there. You can't hide from them. They find you because they are *in you*. All you can do is say, "Hey, I see you. I feel you. And it doesn't matter. I am still doing _____ anyway."

Jordan Peterson, a Canadian professor of psychology, said, "Anything worth doing is worth doing badly, so start by doing it badly, but do it." You will make mistakes. The process is about moving past them and learning from them. Mistakes are an essential part of every learning process. While we often just learn about people's success, I think we miss an important message when we don't hear about the mistakes that occurred before and during the process.

Persistence and Patience

Persistence and patience. How many times did you fall (fail) before you learned to walk or ride a bicycle? What if you never got up? The only difference was you didn't know enough to be afraid. You didn't have nagging doubts. Oh, and you had lots of encouragement.

Many years ago, I came across the following quote by Calvin Coolidge.

START

I remember where I was standing the first time I read it. It resonated with me immediately, and I thought, *That's it. That is truly what it takes—persistence. I can do that.* I have, on many occasions, had to remind myself of the power of persistence.

"Nothing in the world can take the place of persistence. Talent will not, nothing is more common than unsuccessful men and women with talent. Genius will not; unrewarded genius is almost a proverb. Education will not; the world is full of educated derelicts. Persistence and determination alone are omnipotent. The slogan 'Press On' has solved and will always solve the problems of the human race."

~ Calvin Coolidge, the 30th President of the United States

Like many businesspeople, I tried direct mail to market my business and bring in new customers. Initially, the results were poor, but I kept at it. I used to recoil when someone said to me, "Direct mail, I tried that once." Once isn't enough. Twice, even three times, is not enough. In direct mail marketing, the rule is it takes seven contacts in eighteen months before your audience begins to recognize you. To that end, for my business, I will mail 50,000 pieces locally, 1,000 per week (two weeks off around the December holidays). What is the theme? Persistence. It is said that eighty percent of salespeople never return after an initial rejection. Yet statistics show that often the sale is made on the fourth or fifth attempt. Rejection sucks, but often it is the path to success. With each rejection, you learn something; you pick yourself up, you grow, and move forward.

Think about J.K. Rowling, an unemployed single mom whose first work, *Harry Potter and the Philosopher's Stone*, was rejected twelve times. Bestseller *Chicken Soup for the Soul* by Jack Canfield and Victor Mark Hanson was rejected more than fifty times. What about Sly Stallone? No one wanted to produce *Rocky*. They said it was stupid, and I'll bet the producers who said that are sorry now. Sly just kept going back until finally, someone agreed to do it. Success is about failing, rejection, adjusting your approach, and trying again.

Here are a few more examples of persistence and patience:

- Michael Jordan missed more than 9,000 shots in his career, lost almost 300 games, took a potential game-winning shot twenty-six times . . . and missed. His take was, "I've failed over and over and over again in my life. And that is why I succeed."
- Walt Disney's first business, Laugh-o-Gram Studios, went bankrupt due to his lack of ability to run a successful business. He was once fired from a Missouri newspaper for "not being creative enough."
- And what about Bob Snyder's podcast? Oh, you never heard of him. That's because he quit right before it became super popular.

There is never a guarantee that persistence will work, so let's not be Pollyanna-ish about it. But here's the reality; if you don't try more than once, that is, again and again, if you don't persist, you have little to no chance at all. Given the statistics and the odds of being more successful on the second, third, fourth, fifth, or tenth attempt, why shouldn't you keep going? I always felt I wasn't the brightest bulb in the chandelier, but I sure could outlast the other bulbs.

Remember, success is a process. As Epictetus said, "No great thing is created suddenly." Greatness comes from continuously learning and doing.

START

> It's the constant and determined effort that breaks down all resistance and sweeps away all obstacles.
> ~ Claude M. Bristol

If you are unfamiliar with Claude Bristol, check out the YouTube video with comedian Phillis Diller on Bristol's book, *The Magic of Believing*. In his book, he brings home the importance of beliefs and believing in yourself. Diller said, "Reading his book gave me the courage to start my career." Diller, perhaps unknown to younger people, provides a good lesson, too. In the 1960s, she became—at age thirty-seven—a pioneer in stand-up comedy, a field that had very few women. It was her persistence and a desire for continual improvement that made her a comedic legend.

Remember; dreams without action are simply wishes... daydreams . . . fantasies . . . pipe dreams . . . hope. Hope is not a plan. That's right. Hope is not a plan. Hoping everything will work is not the same as a plan. A plan is tangible, one you can see, touch, read, post, and act on.

Life belongs to the doers—not to the dreamers, thinkers, or wishers, but to the doers. You need to *do*. START, even if it's not perfect. Just keep on doing, keep learning, and adjusting. Stop the excuses. Next time you say, "I wish," stop and think:

- Do I really wish for or want that?
- What am I willing to do to get it?
- When do I start? (How about now!)
- What is the first small step?
- What is the next small step?
- How will I be accountable?
- Who will hold me accountable?

Act now while the iron is hot! The step-by-step process I detail in this book may not be easy. Yet, if you want to change your life, then commit these words to memory when the going gets tough, when you want to quit, when you don't feel like Starting: *Suck It Up, Cupcake,* and smile to yourself! Okay, are you ready? Go ahead and say it to yourself, "Yes, I am ready now. I am ready to start!" Move forward while your emotions are on a high.

Do this now. Get a notebook and start writing your action plan. The physical act of writing will connect your body and mind. It will help you get clear and stay connected to your goal. And always, always remember; if you fall seven times, get up eight.

It rarely gets easier. You just get stronger. No matter what happens, you are learning, growing, and becoming more valuable, more confident.

You *can* do it. START!

"The miracle isn't that I finished. The miracle is that I had the courage to start."
~ John Bingham, *an American congressman, and ambassador*

Tools

- Write on paper what you want; writing will connect you to your goals.
- Keep paper and pen with you at all times.
- Take small steps
- Keep going

31

2

The "F" Word

> "You can have almost anything you want if you are willing
> to give up your time, money, energy, and your fears."
> ~ Dennis McCurdy

It's never polite to use the "F" word, but I've always been a bit of a rule-breaker, so I am just going to say it: FEAR.

We can sugarcoat it, dance around it, and continue researching it all we want, but most of the lost potential in the world comes from our fears. Never underestimate the power and effects of fear in your life, both to keep you safe and to keep you stuck.

Fear is a funny thing. For starters, we all seem to think other people aren't afraid, and in return, they think we aren't either. But we are all afraid—from the CEOs of major corporations to the custodian. The other funny thing about fear is that even though we know what we need to do, we let our fears sabotage us through doubt, anxiety, and worry. We know what's going on; we know it is just fear, but we still let it happen, and we deny, suppress, or run away from that which scares us. Why? Because it sucks to be afraid. So we try to hide, deny and cover up our fears, often by blaming or making excuses. That is why it is very important to pay attention to your excuses. They are usually telling you a story about you, your doubts, and your fears.

"When you run away from your fears, they get bigger.
When you run towards them, they get smaller."
~ Barry Neil Kaufman, founder of *The Option Institute*

The first step to moving past our fears is to stop denying them. Begin to embrace and understand them. Any time you shine a light on something, it gives you clarity, helps you see that "thing" for what it is—fear. You can spend your whole life imagining ghosts, worrying about the pathway to the future, or projecting fear onto things that may never happen. Or you can move toward it and through it and grow. All you have is this moment, and the decisions you make in this moment will be based on courage or fear.

"If you have to eat a frog, don't look at it too long."
~ Mark Twain

The reality is we are far more controlled by fear than we realize or admit. Most of us are not even aware that we are afraid because we don't pay attention and take responsibility for what's going on inside of us. And most people don't understand that our beliefs create our fears.

"Everything you have ever wanted is on the other side of
FEAR."
~ George W. Adair, co-founder of *The Atlanta Street
Railway Company*

We all want the same basic things. We all want to be liked, loved, happy, and healthy, to be safe, have fun, and enjoy life. We are afraid of not being loved, not being liked, or being judged as bad, odd, different, or not acceptable. We are afraid to show our imperfections. We are here today because, as early humans, we focused on two things: staying alive and being part of the tribe.

Thousands of years ago, if you were not part of the tribe, you likely were simply dead meat, that is, sabertoothed tiger food. We needed each other for protection—for safety, and we still do. Even today, we need a tribe—other people. One of the worst punishments for a human being is exile, banishment, and having no contact with others. Being viewed as an outcast, laughed at, or seen as different or weird is hard for people and can feel hurtful. That's why we all work so hard to fit in. There is nothing wrong with that as long as it isn't crushing your potential. By the way, the marketing and advertising industry, as well as religion and government know this better than anyone and use fear to control us.

"Fear will always be a player in your life, but you get to
decide how much."
~ Jim Carrey's commencement speech at Maharishi
University

So, let me ask you this; is fear writing the script for your life? If so, don't feel bad. It does for most of us, even when we think or pretend it doesn't. Now is the time to wake up, Suck It Up Cupcake, pick up your pen, and start writing your own life script. The reality is that what we truly want most in life usually doesn't happen because our fears and beliefs don't support what we say we want. We are quite creative in making up fears and then denying we have them. So we need to learn to pay attention, to listen to ourselves on a very deep level. And if we do begin to make changes, the world can become our oyster—or something else wonderful if you don't like oysters.

Most people choose not to take action in their lives until their backs are against the wall—and I am talking about everything from health to love and wealth. We often wait to take action only when a new, bigger fear trumps the old one; for example, a salesperson's fear of being fired outweighs the fear of making cold calls.

So, what are you afraid of? Failing? Rejection? What Other People Think? Being successful? Being found out? Fear creates self-defeating behaviors like procrastination. Fear sabotages us far beyond what we realize.

Fear is the silent killer of your goals and dreams. Fear shuts down the motivational part of your brain. We are afraid to want what we want because we're afraid we will fail. And so, we become afraid to want; we let unreal fears keep us from moving toward our dreams. It is a form of madness.

"Fear is that little darkroom where negatives are developed."
~ Michael Prichard

Fear still freezes me, still looms in my life, still keeps me stuck if I allow it to. What I do know is that when I face fear, analyze it, and move toward it, I move forward.

So, let's dig deeper into what fear is and where it comes from. Did you know that all fears are learned? Yes, all except for the fear of falling, the fear of loud noises (the startle response), and the fear of insurance agents.

There is another fear type—mythical fear—fears we create in our minds based on past experience, half-truths, myths, or urban legends we were told. These experiences may be so painful that we do not want to have them happen again. At such pressure points in our development, we build in behaviors to help us cope, and we can shut down. The problems arise when these behaviors are no longer useful. Yet, in some situations, our mind triggers the old experience. This happens in an instant, so fast we don't even know it on a conscious level. This is why paying attention and self-reflection are extremely important. These mythical fears lead to self-defeating behavior. Never doubt the power of your imagination to create fears that will keep you stuck.

The next time you find yourself feeling fear, ask yourself these questions:

- Does my response to fear alleviate or perpetuate it?
- Is it really that bad, or is it just my imagination running away with me?
- What is the worst that could happen?
- Will I be better off if I push through it?
- Can I handle it?

Barry Neil Kaufman, the founder of The Option Institute, says, "All fear has a target. There is no fear of the unknown." He explains that we have a deep-seated "something" we base our fears on—something with physical or emotional depth, depending on the type of fear. If you dig deep enough, it will reveal itself. When we experience a fear sensation, we stop and think about what triggered it? What are we thinking about?

Fear is learned through experience. Let's look at an example. Parents take their three-year-old daughter to the zoo. They walk around all day looking at giraffes, buffalo, zebras, and monkeys—all kinds of animals. As they come around a corner, the little girl sees a huge cage with a massive and beautiful orange and black Bengal tiger lying there sunning itself. What does the three-year-old want to do? She wants to pet the kitty. She has no fear of Bengal tigers. To her, it is merely a very big kitty, not unlike the one she has at home. That fear, and it's a useful one, must be learned.

Unfortunately, there are many unfounded fears that are learned in the first seven years of life, when our minds were the most malleable. We learned them from our family, school, and society. These fear-based beliefs are rooted deeply in our subconscious minds. They run on automatic pilot, so deep that we don't even realize they are there. If you pay attention to the things you do, and particularly things you won't do, you will see them in action.

When you anticipate failure, you manufacture (imagine) fear and set up a self-defeating behavior cycle. Anxiety and worry cause you to experience failure in advance. This is something to monitor. Once you conclude that you will fail, you unconsciously put into operation the very behaviors that bring about your failure. In other words, you hold back your efforts to succeed. This is called a self-fulfilling prophecy.

Here is how that works. People might set themselves up for failure at work by coming in late, not fully engaging in what they're doing, missing deadlines, not paying attention, distracting themselves or others with Facebook, YouTube, idle gossip, and other things. Why would fear of failure cause someone to behave in a way that ensures failure? By ensuring failure, a person will rationalize, *I never really failed because I never really tried to succeed.* People who fear failure choose to lose by forfeit rather than show up for the game and take a risk.

The "F" Word

Fear of Failure and Success

Your greatest nemesis is you. When you fear following your own journey to becoming the person you want to be, it is usually because you are afraid to fail. We fear what others will say or think about us. And yes, sometimes more than we realize, we are afraid to succeed. What might happen if you really succeed? You may have to move, leave friends, or maybe your friends can no longer do the same things as you. Some people may say not-so-nice things about you. Some will talk behind your back, even make up stuff, which sucks! However, know this. It isn't about you, it is about them. I have found that if you acted like a jerk before you were successful, you'll continue to do so; if you act nice, that behavior continues, too.

As for failing and making mistakes, it is important to understand that from each failure or mistake comes valuable lessons and experience. After all, isn't that what experience is? Learning from mistakes and growing? The only big mistake is not learning or giving up and quitting too soon.

Success Formula

T+MM+L+TA=S
Try + Make Mistakes + Learn + Try Again = Success
Repeat

My earlier years found me working as a real estate agent. During that time, I made a lot of mistakes, and I failed many times. During the first fourteen months of my venture into the real estate business, I spent a lot of time reading and studying books authored by successful real estate gurus and investors, like Albert Lowery and William Nickerson, who wrote *How to Become a Millionaire Investing in Real Estate.* During that time, I dabbled in several areas of the business, including building, marketing, accounting, taxes, and learning how businesses operate, all of which I knew nothing about. I was on the "learn as you go" plan. Just like writing my books and developing my workshops, I knew nothing. I just started and analyzed what went wrong and what went right. More importantly, I learned a lot, and there were many small successes.

Over many years, I continued to try new things—to learn and grow, in real estate, insurance, finance, and writing. I'm often asked what created this metamorphosis. There are a number of parts to this answer:

1. I know how to work, and work is essential.
2. I was open to saying yes to opportunities. Opportunities are always available, but we tend to shut our eyes to them. I managed to keep my eyes open.
3. I possessed an immeasurable faith in myself (sprinkled with doubt) and a "find a way" attitude.
4. I realized that if one person could do it, then so could I, and I chose to learn from the people who had achieved what I was seeking to achieve.
5. Rather than spending days, weeks, months, or years planning the execution of my vision, I chose to start.
6. I viewed mistakes as steppingstones to success. Every mistake was a learning experience that helped me reach my goals and increase my value. I never liked failing; I just avoided staying stuck. I have learned it's better to push forward.
7. I learned to ask questions. People are more than willing to provide help and advice, what I call free education. They will give you all the information you need and more. Just ask! And listen.

Every person and experience is our teacher, whether it is an idea, a lesson to learn, or a lesson on what to avoid.

Failure and success are kissing cousins. Everything we know today, *everything*, came about because of someone's failure. For example, the first caveman who stuck his hand in fire learned, do that, and you get burned. And now we know, "Don't stick your hand in the fire."

"If you are not prepared to be wrong,
you will never come up with anything original."
~ Sir Kenneth Robinson

We are usually wrong more than we are right, and some of us, me included, keep repeating our mistakes over and over again. The path to success is littered with our mistakes and failures, aka, lessons. If we aren't failing at least a little, we aren't moving forward. That is the same as being stuck.

In the movie *Groundhog Day,* Bill Murray repeatedly relived the same day. Notably, he learned something each day and applied those lessons. The movie ended with this dour and cynical person finally getting it. He moved on to the next day as a success.

Ralph Waldo Emerson wrote, "Do not be too timid and squeamish about your actions. All life is an experiment. The more experiments you make, the better. What if you do fall and get rolled in the dirt once or twice? Up again, you shall never be so afraid of a tumble."

Go ahead, take a tumble. I dare you! Don't be so afraid of your mistakes and failures; just learn from them and *grow.*

"Success is 99% failure."
~ Soichiro Honda

If you listen to anyone successful, they will talk fondly, almost joyously, about many of their setbacks, lapses, and failures because they understand those were part of their process, and it's behind them. Success seems to be a matter of hanging on. It's all about finding a way to keep yourself going and remembering to give yourself a little pleasure and fun along the way. Doing nothing, risking nothing, creates nothing and failure by default.

Fearless Quiz

On a scale of 1-5, with 1 being the minimum level demonstrated and 5 being the maximum level, indicate to what level each of the following statements describes you, most often.

I take on new challenges frequently	1	2	3	4	5
I set goals and work toward achieving them	1	2	3	4	5
I keep my goals in plain sight	1	2	3	4	5
I have an accountability system to track my goal activity	1	2	3	4	5
I speak up when something is wrong	1	2	3	4	5
I raise my hand at seminars	1	2	3	4	5
I invest time, energy and money in my personal development	1	2	3	4	5
I have a mentor or coach	1	2	3	4	5
I ask for what I want and need	1	2	3	4	5
I know that I create my fears and I can change them	1	2	3	4	5
I stand up for myself	1	2	3	4	5
I push through my fears and take action and quickly	1	2	3	4	5
I do not accept poor behavior or results	1	2	3	4	5
I avoid excuses & blaming	1	2	3	4	5
Total					

My score

14 to 20

50 to 70

35

When Virgin Galactic founder Richard Branson's rocket plane crashed, he vowed to keep going. He was seven years behind his schedule to take civilians into space, but he vowed to keep trying.

The path to success is seldom an unimpeded, high-speed romp. The roadside is home to those who hit a bump and decide the journey is too tough, so they pitch a tent and camp where they are. If that were the rule, Lincoln would never have been president, there would be no polio vaccine, Apple wouldn't exist, and we would never have set foot on the moon.

The greatest successes I know are people who had to battle, overcome, and persevere. These are people who kept stepping up to the plate and running the bases of life with determination.

If you have a desire, a passion for something, most likely you can do it. The most important thing is to get it out of your head and make it a reality. Start taking action toward your goal, desire, passion, or dream.

I have a friend, Charlie, who drives to Boston every other Sunday night for five minutes on stage at Dick Doherty's House of Comedy. He didn't go to comedy school; he just decided to start writing comedy, to practice, and ultimately, to perform. That's what it takes. Action. How many people do that? Better question; how many people want to do that? Will you do that? Will you do something that moves you in the direction you truly want to go?

Most people are shocked when they find out I didn't go to college. Well, full disclosure, I did go to a local community college for one semester. It wasn't for me. Don't get me wrong. I really enjoy and want to learn. I just want to learn what I want. So instead of going to college, I decided to go into business and learn as much as I could by reading books, talking with people, and making lots and lots and lots of mistakes.

It was the same with selling insurance. Often, the first time I went out on a big account, I blew it. I didn't get a commission, but I sure got an education. The next time I was more prepared. You can be successful at almost anything if you're willing to spend the time and occasionally get a little egg on your face.

Life is about trial and error. Actually, more trial than error. But each time you make a mistake, each time something goes wrong, you learn. That's the most effective way to truly become successful. As one of my mentors said, "You can't learn to ride a bicycle in a seminar." Think about that. Could you sit in a room and learn how to ride a bicycle? No, you need to be on the bicycle, to feel the fear, the wobbliness when learning to balance, turn, and brake. You may fall, and when you do, you learn by getting up and getting back on.

It is the same with becoming fearless or fearing less. You need to move toward your fears. I know it is scary, and it can suck. That is why you need to take a really deep breath and Suck It Up, Cupcake.

People often begin with the hypothesis that they will never succeed, that failure will be costly, so they look for every shred of evidence to justify giving up. That is known as confirmation bias; we seek information to support what we want to believe.

Jim Carrey said, "My father could have been a great comedian, but he didn't believe that was possible for him, and so he made a conservative choice. Instead, he got a safe job as an accountant, and when I was twelve years old, he was let go from that safe job, and our family had to do whatever we could to survive.

"I learned many great lessons from my father. Not the least of which was that you can fail at what you don't want, so you might as well take a chance on doing what you love."

To that, I will add, either do what you love or love what you do; it is a mindset.

Fear of Rejection

Human beings need connection and acceptance, and we will do almost anything to satisfy that need. Think about this. We have always needed others to survive. From the time we're born, there's nothing we can do except depend on our parents and caregivers. If they didn't, we would die. So connection is, in a way, protection from death. Nowadays, it isn't only lions and tigers and bears, oh my, that threaten us—it's paper tigers, social tigers, and media tigers.

The need to belong is strong and will cause us to do things that are not necessarily good for us. Once we get in a strong group, it has an influence on us, and it may be difficult to leave. We fear losing the connection, being exiled and banished. Pirates would maroon sailors on an island; some religious organizations do this by excommunicating someone from the church. Children do this in their groups or cliques in schools.

This is why we tread so carefully around many situations, why we acquiesce, even when we don't want to or it's not in our best interest.

So what can you do? Unfortunately, there aren't any magic pills. You must confront your fear and desensitize yourself. I see this all the time in Toastmasters International, the largest organization in the world dedicated to helping people become better communicators and leaders through public speaking.

I've seen individuals who could stand in front of the group for twenty seconds, then walk quickly back to their seat, trembling. Some attend one or two meetings and never return, unable to confront their fears, even in a supportive, positive environment. Others will stay and six months later, we can't shut them up! They confronted their fears and slowly became desensitized, courageous, and began to soar. Before Albert Ellis became a world-famous psychologist, he had crippling social anxiety, especially when asking women out on dates. To solve this problem, he decided he would go to the Bronx Botanical Gardens every day for a month and talk with women. He approached more than 130 women that summer. About thirty walked away, yet he spoke at length with the rest. However, only one woman agreed to go on a date with him, and she never showed up. Ellis took a tumble in the dirt more than a hundred times and overcame his fear. His anxiety problem led to the technique now known as exposure therapy—the active confrontation of a particular fear. Ellis learned you must face your fear regardless of the outcome, not internalize it and beat yourself up. We cannot control outcomes. We can only control our behavior and actions.

Fear and rejection are almost synonymous. Remember the childhood song that went, *Nobody likes me, everybody hates me. Think I'll go and eat some worms?* We used to sing it by the nightly campfire at Boy Scout Camporees. Rejection can make us do strange things, and make us cringe. What will make you cringe? Even after forty years of selling, I can, at times, get squeamish making cold calls or walking into a business. Cold calls and walk-ins equal rejection. I attend many networking groups where no one networks. They find a safe person or corner. They hide out and lose out.

With our irrational self-talk, we invent the necessity instead of the preference of being approved by others. By necessity, I mean we have to have the approval of others. Preference means we would like it, but do not necessarily need it. We make their rejection "terrible" instead of "unfortunate" or "Oh well." We obsessively, compulsively demand that acceptance by others, including our partners equals our worth as a person. *It does not!*

What we do to ourselves before and after the rejection can cause the greatest damage, usually because it is self-inflicted. So here is a really good place to stop your irrational thinking and to START to take control of your thoughts and emotions. As with everything in life, it is our thoughts that drive our actions, our emotions. That is why paying attention is so important. How will you deal with it? Have a rejection plan.

I like to remind myself of something Jack Falvey, a nationally known sales trainer, said. It's a good mantra whether you are in sales, customer service, asking people for things, or asking for a date. Jack says, "Some will, some won't, so what. *Next!*"

The What Other People Think Disease

"Acceptance is the most significant need of human beings."
~ William James

Why are we so concerned with what other people think? Is this because we need other people to survive? Is it from our childhood because we knew we had to please our parents or thought we did to get what we needed or wanted? Where does it come from, and why does it affect us, even though we are supposed to be grown-up, adult, rational human beings? Hint: we are not as rational as we believe we are.

Often, we allow the need to be part of a "herd" to hold us back. We are far more concerned about WOPT than with what we want. Let me say that again; we are more concerned about "What Other People Think" than with what we want.

Stop giving a crap about *what other people think*. Stop worrying about what other people think and start thinking about what you want. Take a step toward self-fulfillment. The people on the sidelines (waiting to see if you fail) are just spectators in life instead of living life. And the higher you go, the more you will get rejected. And guess what? Rejection with persistence becomes success. If you open yourself up to the world, the world opens up to you. Rejection can be useful! See it as a learning tool and remember not to take it personally.

Perfection

This is a tough one for me. As my daughter likes to say, "I am a lazy perfectionist." In other words, we want things to be perfect, but we get tired, bored, or take on too much. We give up before we get there.

Our fear of not being perfect is yet another self-imposed obstacle. We need to remember one very important thing. We are all perfectly imperfect. Many people are trying to find the road to perfection only to realize it is a dead-end street. There should be no shame in admitting our mistakes. When we admit a mistake, we are saying we are wiser than we were before. The search for perfection is a detour from the mission to create meaning and value.

Take, for instance, this book. It won't be perfect. Who knows if people will like it or gain anything from it? I really hope they do, yet some may critique it negatively. To those critics, I always liked the expression, "My crappy book is better than the one that you never wrote." Done is better than perfect. Many people talk about writing a book, but I did it. Granted, my writing, spelling, and clarity are not always world-class; that's why there are editors and proofreaders. Yet, there are some people could not wait to tell me about errors in my previous book, *Find A Way*. Once a person told me he couldn't focus on content if there were a typo. I told him I hoped he was receiving counseling. So, I'll repeat: the search for perfection is a detour from the mission to create meaning.

Writing is about ideas, conveying thoughts and messages; editing is about making all that better but rarely perfect.

Some people would rather find flaws than find their futures. When people tell me they found seven typos in one of my books, I tell them there are actually twelve, which drives them crazy. Don't misunderstand. I'm not seeking forgiveness for my errors, only tolerance for being human.

Sometimes I think the biggest mistake I make, that many of us make, is expecting ourselves to be perfect, to be superhuman. I've yet to meet anyone who fits the bill. I've met some very sharp people who do a great job, and still, they are not perfect. There are a lot of not-perfect, average people who are quite successful. I think that's because it's all about making mistakes, falling off the horse, and getting back on. Said another way, "Screw up, then get up." Make that your motto.

Remind yourself that you are a perfectly imperfect human being. And work at doing what you can, continually improving. Also, it is important to realize that if beating yourself up worked, you would be perfect by now, so go easy.

Fear of Success

The "F" Word

Sometimes when we are on the way to being successful, we sabotage ourselves by allowing self-imposed obstacles to get in our way just so we can have an excuse for our failure. Yet if we succeed, even with those obstacles, our success will seem all the more impressive. After all, success has to be grueling, right? Wrong! It might be work, but we tend to make it even more challenging for ourselves by creating diversions because we don't feel we deserve success.

You will be surprised by how many people are afraid of success. I remember telling my friend and mentor, Frank, how much I wanted to earn. When I told him the amount, he insisted that I could earn about fifty percent more than I proposed. I was shocked. I thought, *Is he crazy? No one is worth that much money. Only crooks make that much money.* This is an example of how our brain works and how, with lightning speed, old negative beliefs can jump us. I also noticed that as I reached certain levels of income success, I would sometimes slow down, goof off, put obstacles in my way. These actions reflected my personal belief about the type of person who earns a lot of money. It is self-defeating thinking.

Most often, our hesitancy is based on a faulty belief system combined with our lack of self-worth. Frank helped me understand and embrace the fact that not everyone knew what I knew and had my level of knowledge, aka, business value. It's always about improving yourself to give more value to others. Even so, it was scary to acknowledge, no less accept. I did take it in, and as I did, I felt myself begin to literally vibrate. I *was* worth a lot more, financially speaking. And so are you if you develop your skills, nurture your potential, increase your value, and let yourself succeed!

"Comfort makes cowards of us all."
~ Mark Twain

We are taught to desire comfort. In fact, for many people, being comfortable is their only goal. While comfort can be a good thing, it can also be a crutch. We use it as an excuse. It is the propaganda of the average, spouted by the average, the media, and institutions. We spend a great deal of time organizing our lives around avoiding discomfort. Nobody likes to be uncomfortable yet accepting some short-term discomfort can allow us to have long-term gains. So, START taking risks. Don't worry about mistakes and failures. Instead, think about what you're giving up when you don't try—when you are unwilling to make mistakes. Think about the life you're not living and the happiness you're foregoing as you merely exist in the safety of your comfort zone. Give yourself permission to survive doing it wrong, making mistakes, yet recovering from them and growing to be your better self.

Growth is about trusting your wisdom and being brave. It's about following your heart, not the herd, even if everyone else thinks you're crazy. It's about knowing that you have something to give the world and not stopping until you figure out what that is and then doing it.

We run on emotions. It's natural. However, try to live by the ABCs:

Action
Bravery
Consistency

One of the hardest things to do, and one thing we need to do, is to let go so we can grow. We get stuck in comfort zones doing the same old things. But we can't grow if we don't try something different. Let go of the things that are holding you back. Let go of:

The "F" Word

- Negative people
- Poor workers
- Poor work habits
- Wasting time
- Projects you will never complete
- Trying to please everyone
- Fearing change
- Living in the past
- Putting yourself down
- Overthinking
- Trying to be perfect
- Fear

Limiting beliefs, those thoughts, fears, and doubts you harbor deep inside that surface anytime you want to try something new; you are faced with challenges or obstacles.

There is always a cost when you allow fear, judgment, and lack of courage to run your life. Fear can blind you to opportunities in ways you don't realize. The cost isn't always money. The cost can be the loss of love, friendship, relationships, joy, health, and more. "Do the thing you fear, and the death of fear is certain," Emerson wrote. Yes, there is no magic pill— just courage, so build your courage muscle.

Get in the habit of asking yourself, "What is the worst that can happen," and "Can I handle it, even if I don't like it?" Acknowledging your feelings does not mean you are a wimp or can't do something. It just lets you know you have them, that you are responsible, and that you have the power to take charge.

"Life shrinks or expands based on your courage."
~ Anais Nin

Fear is a shadow of the mind held by ignorance and darkness. When you hold it up to the light and examine it, it will shrink and may even disappear. Don't let fear push you around. Fear is a bully. And like all bullies, it doesn't like people to stand up to it because it takes away their power. No one can control your thoughts, or your fears, except you.

The following is another excerpt from Jim Carrey's commencement address at Maharishi University:

All you have are the decisions you make at this moment, which are based on love or fear. So many of us choose a path of fear disguised as practicality. What we really want seems impossibly out of reach and so ridiculous to expect that we never dare to ask the Universe for it. You can ask the Universe for it. Life doesn't happen to you; it happens for you. It is about letting the Universe know what you want and working toward it while letting go of how it comes to you.

Why not take a chance on faith, not religion, not hope, but faith? I don't believe in hope. Hope is a beggar. Hope walks through the fire and faith leaps over it. You are ready and able to do beautiful things in this world. You will always have two choices: love or fear. Choose love, and don't ever let fear turn you against your playful heart.

Action is the Cure for FEAR

- Do it scared
- Do it unsure
- Do it uncomfortable
- Do it often
- Do it

Stop Looking for Obstacles

I recently told a successful sales trainer I wanted to start a training company for professionals. He immediately brought up all kinds of obstacles I'd have to overcome.

When I hung up the phone, I thought, *Wow! I was looking for the positive, for how this may work, not how it might not work!* I didn't expect it to be easy. I didn't expect it to go quickly. I knew there would be obstacles. But this was something I wanted to try, something that would improve my business and help my staff grow. I knew that if I didn't give it a go, I'd always regret it. What if it failed? I will have learned what works and what doesn't.

All too often, we focus on obstacles or manufacture them, so we don't even have to try. And yes, change and challenges are scary. So, I chose to focus on what I wanted and how I could get it. There will always be bumps and obstacles; that's life. Stop looking for obstacles and start looking for advantages and opportunities.

I believe that every time you try, you learn. Even if you fail *you* become more valuable. Believe in and know your value, your worth. Always remember the truth will set you free, but first, it will scare you and then piss you off.

Take a few minutes and think about your fears using the worksheet below. It's scary. You need to be honest, really honest. Think not only about the fear, but when it happens, how you let it stop you, self-imposed obstacles, and what action you can take, for example, smaller steps, having support close by, talking it through with someone, or sucking it up cupcake. Take a minute or two and complete the exercise below, *What Are My Fears.*

What Are My Fears

What is the fear?	When does it happen?	What sort of obstacles do I tend to impose?	What step or action can I take now?

Tools
1. Start Small
2. Get support (never underestimate the power of support)
3. Ask for help

Beliefs

Most often, it isn't failure that stops us; it is our beliefs about failure. We all look at life through our belief system. We have perceptions of everything created by our beliefs and the meaning we give to what happens. Often, our experiences have little to do with what is happening in our lives, yet everything to do with what is happening within us.

Aaron Helmsley, trainer, speaker, and creator of the training program *The Psychology of Persuasion*, told of his experience with his family. "Every time we were on a family drive and my father saw someone drive by in a new Cadillac, he would always say, 'There goes a crook.'" The implication was anyone successful must have been doing something illegal, rather than setting goals, taking risks, working hard, and being persistent. Well, that's a load of crap to dump on your children. Maybe he should have said, "I am too afraid to set goals and go after them."

I often give this example in my workshops. Suppose when you were young, at family events, someone would always bring up Uncle Charlie, who lost all of his money in real estate. The message you received was, "Don't buy real estate. It's a dangerous investment." To your young mind, it served as a cautionary tale. The problem, however, was that you only heard part of the story. You did not hear that Uncle Charlie was a drinker and gambler, that he had to sell his properties at a low price to pay off gambling debts.

OF COURSE I STILL BELIEVE. I ALSO BELIEVE THAT "SUCCESS IS BAD", "NICE PEOPLE ARE POOR", AND "WEALTHY PEOPLE ARE CROOKS"

Think about it. Do you have any beliefs based on half-truths, distorted information, unrealistic values, urban legends, or myths? Can you see how they create certain perceptions and shape your reality? If so, know that you can challenge them, change your reality, and not be disabled by such limiting beliefs. You can't repair if you are not aware. So pay attention.

Understanding that you can choose the meaning of the events in your life gives you tremendous power. Power to change the quality of your experiences, the quality of your results, and the quality of your life. As the saying goes, if you are not failing at least a little, you probably aren't moving forward. You are merely treading water.

When I reached a net worth of one million dollars at age 36, I developed an inner struggle, so much so that I was going to strike the word "millionaire" from this book because I get uncomfortable saying that about myself. I get the same feeling about saying I am a writer, even though this is my third book. I have also written over 300 articles, many speeches, and workshops. After all, who am I to have achieved any type of success? Who am I to have the credibility to offer advice to others? These thoughts stood in my way. Even today, these thoughts can sometimes creep in and create doubt. As much as we often believe we cannot be successful, even when we succeed, a cloud can roll in and cause us to second guess ourselves and our value. The real answer for me is I worked hard and took lots of risks, tried new things, made a ton of mistakes. I still do. Most importantly, every day, I work and learn.

Self-doubt is one of the largest obstacles we *all* face— an obstacle entirely based on our beliefs. We could *all* benefit from developing the "why-not-me" attitude because there is no valid reason why it shouldn't be you. You are just as worthy as those who reached the success level for which you are striving. The truth is that you and I are not any better or worse than someone else; people with great accomplishments are not necessarily amazing, out-of-this-world individuals. They are just everyday people who wake up in the morning and make a conscious decision to take action in alignment with their goals.

Your job is to continue to discover your strengths, weaknesses, and fears and develop into a more valuable person at all levels. Are you focusing on your strengths or your weaknesses? Are you letting one area of weakness dominate your life? My philosophy is to find your strengths and find ways to use them, to improve and grow them and to reduce and minimize any negative impact from your weaknesses. As Jim Rohn said, "Don't wish things were different. Wish you were better." Make that happen by using your strengths, by improving yourself. There is no other way. Too often, we assume that we can't do something. We assume someone else is better than we are and give up or don't try. Most likely, that "better" person is just like you, but maybe they practice more, study, or work harder. You only need to measure progress in yourself and not against others. As Aristotle said, "The hardest victory is victory over self."

Another mistake is turning successful people into heroes. But really, they're people just like you and me. The difference is they are people who keep getting up and taking one or two steps more, use their time better, and push through their doubts and fears. It is vital to understand that this is the key—for the most part, everyone is just like you. They often are not smarter or more talented. They decided what they wanted and took the time to develop it. Just because you are a cook today doesn't mean you can't own a chain of restaurants tomorrow if you take the time to change your beliefs and develop new skills. Look at the story of David Thomas, the founder of Wendy's.

Dave started working in restaurants at age twelve. Later, he quit high school and entered the Army at eighteen. After completing his military service, he worked in a local restaurant in Fort Wayne, Indiana, where he met and began working for Colonel Sanders of KFC. In the mid-60s, he was sent to Columbus, Ohio, to rescue four failing KFC restaurants, which he did. After that experience, he sold his shares in KFC back to Colonel Sanders and, the following year, started Wendy's.

You've probably heard the saying, "We are what we eat." But I prefer Alan Weiss's version. "We are what we tell ourselves." People get up in the morning either eager to squeeze opportunity out of another new day or dread a slow, tough crawl through enemy territory. Which are you? How can you begin to change this?

What you put into your head can be more important than what you put into your body. This is not an excuse to load up on Twinkies. Your beliefs about yourself and the labels you give yourself create attitudes about your situation that manifest in your behavior. *The words you use to describe yourself and your behavior are your choice:* hard worker or lucky; perseverant or stubborn; conqueror or defeated; fortunate or unworthy. You control the words, and they control the results of your experiences. Developing a deeper understanding of your beliefs will help you.

Your beliefs—faith in your goals, vision, and *yourself*—are the key difference between wallowing in mediocrity and achieving prosperity. You have the option to work toward them every day—your choice.

> "It ain't so much the things that people know that makes trouble in the world,
> as it is the things that people know that ain't so."
> ~ Mark Twain

Take Action Now

Make a list of your beliefs. Handwrite it because the process takes longer and makes you think deeper. The action connects your body and brain. Do not filter or ignore what you think or feel.

Here is a sample from my list. I want to write a book. The thought or belief:

- Who do you think you are to write a book?
- You didn't go to college.
- You failed English.
- What you have to say isn't important enough.

Get the idea? These are mostly faulty beliefs that fuel fear and doubt. And this is exactly what we often do to ourselves.

Pay attention to such statements beginning with "I am:"

- too old
- too young
- not smart enough
- time-challenged
- too poor
- too short or too tall
- not good enough
- a failure
- afraid I can't have love
- fearful of making a mistake and appearing stupid
- out of opportunities
- not sure if I have choices
- not good in school

I suggest you add or modify the list. Keep a journal of when one of those unhelpful beliefs creep into your life. Keep track of the good stuff, too. Being aware and grateful goes a long way. You need to pay attention to your thoughts, actions, and reactions. It's helpful, too, to create a daily "Gratitude Journal," perhaps entering three things for which you're grateful. Writing about the big stuff such as family and friends is important, but it's also the little things—hot coffee, showers, computers, flowers.

Here are some ways you can flip your beliefs:

- Too old. People my age *are* doing exciting things, such as skydiving, writing books, or starting businesses.
- Too young. I am in the learning stage with lots of time to grow.
- No money. I can find resources. If I need a business or personal coach, I can do their yard work, run errands, walk their dog, wash their car (or whatever you can offer) in exchange for coaching.
- No money II. I can find a partner or investor.

It's Your Choice

You have a choice in every moment of every day as to how you will live your life. It is your choice. It is always your choice.

Yes, it is your choice. You and I have been taught that it isn't and that only serves the belief that we are victims, and it is disempowering. You see, knowing you have choices gives you power. That is why it is important to pay attention to all the self-talk produced from our beliefs, scripts, and the stories we tell ourselves. Many of those stories, the ones that we are holding on to, are the ones that hold us back. Now that we have taken the time to pay attention to our thoughts, we can look deeper into why we have these beliefs and work on changing them.

Listen to Henry Ford, who said, "Whether you think you can or you think you can't, you're right." We can go back even further to the seventeenth century when John Dryden said, "For they can conquer who believe they can." Or all the way back to Virgil in 29 BC, who wrote, *"Possunt quia posse videntu."* [They can because they think they can.] We create what we believe. Understanding this is vital to change.

Michael Jordan, one of the most famous basketball players of all time, became one of the best by taking big risks on his long shots. He did so with confidence because he envisioned taking those shots a thousand times in his mind and in practice. He focused on what he wanted and practiced it—training his mind and reinforcing his belief system. He knew he could make the tough shot because he believed in himself and had visualized his success. When the time came, he didn't overthink it. He just did it.

When we overthink, doubts can creep in. So, write down the following and refer to it during the next few days:

- What do I think about?
- Is it success or failure?
- Being bold or staying safe?
- Do I tell myself I can't, or I can?

We forget that most of our beliefs operate unconsciously because we only recognize or see what's on the surface. The only way we can tell what we believe is by looking around and examining our lives. Observe what you do, what you have created, and understand that by all means, you *are a* creator, and you *are the* creator of your life. You created where and how you live and who you associate with. We tend to go on day after day just thinking things are the way they are because it "just happened" that way. I hear people say all the time, "Things just happen," or "That's just me. That's the way I am." Remember, at one time, you chose to be the way you are, and you can choose something different at any time. Of course, there are things we can't control, such as aging, where we are born and raised, or our family. We can, for the most part, control how well we age. Yes, just go to YouTube and search for an eighty-year-old CrossFit man, woman, or bodybuilder. There, you will see the myth busters, and you can be one too!

So, Suck It Up, Cupcake, and stop screwing yourself. Get to work at living a better life, becoming a better you, one baby step at a time. And remember the Chinese proverb, "It isn't how slow you go. It matters only if you stop."

Unless you begin to seriously question why these things in your life exist, you can never begin to change your life. If you truly want to know why you do what you do, examine your beliefs. It is one of the most powerful things you can do for yourself.

Sometimes as I am laying here at night, I think why am I here, what's my purpose, ...then a voice comes to me SHUTUP I hate that question

When our conscious and subconscious minds are not aligned, it can be difficult to accomplish anything. We become like Sisyphus—damned forever to push a huge boulder up the mountain only to watch it roll to the bottom again and again.

As Daniel Gilbert said, "Disbelieving is hard work." It is hard work because we may have to admit that our beliefs may be holding us back, and we need to change.

Where do all these beliefs come from?

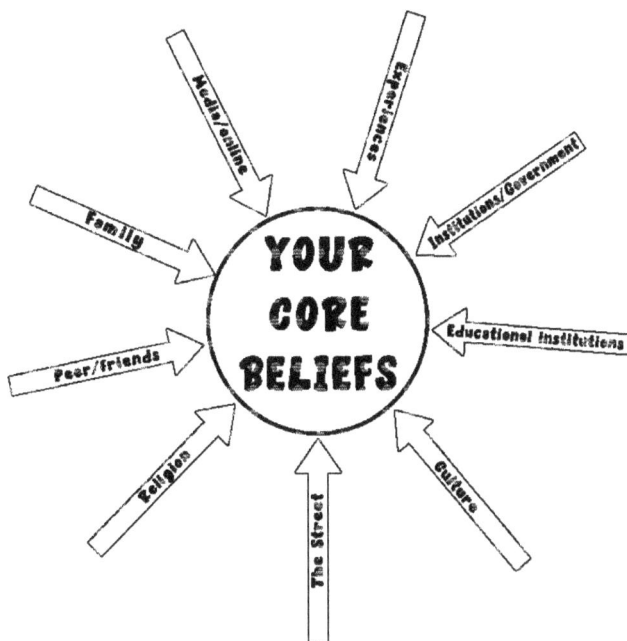

Here is a good example of something most people believe. People believe they can make you (or others) feel something, like anger. The truth is no one can make you feel anything except you. No one has that kind of control over you unless you give it to them, unfortunately this misconception starts early. Do you remember your parents saying, "Don't make your brother (sister) feel bad" or "You make me mad!" Somehow, they had bestowed upon you, at age five, this superpower—you could make others feel! What awesome power! Not really. Yet, all of us bought into it because, at that age, we buy into everything.

Now, let me put a little caution sign up here. Yes, we can do certain things that we believe might evoke a feeling in someone else, but even though we are not responsible for how they feel, it doesn't mean we should be heartless, deliberately mean, or push people's buttons. While we are not responsible for how someone feels, we are responsible for what we say, our actions, and our intentions. Be kind, and always remember, *no one* can make you feel anything *without your permission.*

If someone decided to be deliberately mean, for example, calling you a moron, it is up to you whether you accept and believe their comment. You control the thought and feelings. When that information enters your brain, you could say to yourself, "We just met. How could they know if I was a moron?" Or, you could simply think, *That person has no idea who I am*, or *That person knows my sore spots, but I'm in charge. They are just upset.* Take charge of your thoughts because the power rests with the person in charge of your thoughts, responses, and behaviors, and that is you.

The next time you begin to feel something that may negatively impact you, stop and take a minute. Breathe. Then immediately change the dialogue in your head. Create a better thought. I know this might sound easy, but trust me, it takes practice and patience. Yet it is possible. I would know. I have been selling insurance for over forty years, and I couldn't even begin to try and count the number of people complaining to me about how much they hate insurance. If I had let all those people get to me, I would have given up a long time ago or gone crazy. I finally realized that those individuals didn't understand what I do. They had faulty beliefs about how insurance works. Not only did learning how to cope help me succeed (and maintain my sanity), but it also made me a better advisor by remaining curious and discovering what people's beliefs and needs were and how best to guide them.

Begin to examine the fears you have created, what beliefs they are based on, and which behaviors come into play. Are they protection for your physical safety, or did you create them for your emotional safety? Anytime you begin to feel anxious, worried, nervous, or even excited, take a second to check in with yourself and realize you are creating those emotions. When you start feeling fearful, figure out why because if you don't, the fears will hold you back.

Focusing on the Negative

Your boss calls you into his office. Your doctor calls you at home. What is your first thought? For most of us, our first thought is that we are in trouble or something bad has happened. Similar to our fears, negative thinking is a protective mechanism developed to ensure survival. Our brains are designed to instantly think negatively. We hear a bush rustle. Is it a tiger or a rabbit? The hairs stand up on the back of your neck, and you get a prickly feeling. The reality is that most of us don't need to be worried about a tiger jumping out of the bushes, but we are still programmed to go on high alert just in case.

We tend to focus on the negative rather than the positive. Some people spend their entire lives stuck in negativity. The question for you is, is it useful? We are responsible for our emotions and the beliefs we create; we are not victims. By focusing on goals and moving forward, we become more powerful.

Focusing on the Positive

Many of us believe that if we are wealthy or successful, we will be happy. To a degree, this may be true. However, happiness is a state of mind. It is within your control, and you can choose what it means. You could be happy shoveling chicken shit or miserable on a beach in Hawaii. It's really up to you.

Don't confuse happiness with success. In fact, I think the happier you are on the way to your success, the better off you'll be and more likely to succeed. Happiness is a state of mind.

We create beliefs using a rational filter, and we can invoke hundreds of our beliefs in a millisecond. Remember that we are emotional beings, and our emotions often trump our logic. Embracing positive emotions and maintaining a strong faith in ourselves is vitally important to prevent fear and negative beliefs from hindering our goals.

Hebb's "Law"

Every time you have a thought, you fire specific neurons in your brain. The more you think the same thought, the more you fire those neurons. This is Donald Hebb's "law." He states, "Neurons that fire together, wire together." This repeated "firing" creates strong neural pathways, making it easier to have the same thoughts again and again. That is why change takes time. We need to fire new and better pathways.

Self-talk Park

Imagine strolling through an undiscovered park. As you walk across the grass, you leave no path. But if this walk becomes a daily routine, you begin to create a path. Your brain's neural pathways work in a similar fashion. Each repeated thought automatically deepens and strengthens the neural pathway. In turn, the thoughts, and the behaviors they produce become ingrained whether they are helpful or not. For better results in your life, create a pattern of repeated and positive result-oriented thoughts, which will change your behaviors.

Responsibility

You are the only one who is truly and totally responsible for your life—for what you do, your actions, and what you don't do, inaction. You have the power to change anything if you want to. It may seem difficult at times, but it is up to you to keep on keeping on, even if it sucks for a while.

For example, if you wanted to do 100 free-standing squats every day, that might be hard for you. But what if you could do ten squats? And then, after a week, you added two more. That's twelve. Great! Next week, you increase to fifteen, and then to eighteen. There will come a time when fifty seems like a walk in the park.

The same applies to most things that are challenging. The trick is in starting. Start slow and apply my KISSES principle—Keep It Simple Sustainable Easy and Supported.

The point is, you are in charge, and I know you don't always like to hear it. You need to accept that you can be your own worst enemy. Remember, you control the reins. You are your own prisoner, jailer, and your own savior.

Now is the time to change. Once you get that down, you are at least in the ballpark. Now it is time to stop watching and paying attention to media BS, heroes, flash-in-the-pan success stories, etc. Remember this: most "overnight successes" are ten or twenty years in the making. So, stop being the starving artist, poor musician, depressed or alcoholic writer, or slacking salesperson. It is the person who gets up every day and works toward their goal, whether it is writing a book, starting a business, getting a degree, improving sales, or creating art. All require what Honorée Corder calls "AITS" or Ass In The Seat. In other words, settle down and get started!

Motivational Shower

Many people are under the assumption that they can go to a motivational workshop, read a book, listen to a CD, or watch YouTube, and that's all they ever need to do. "Yup," they say. "I am motivated and reprogrammed for success! Watch me now!" And then, after a few days, weeks, months, or even hours, they fall back into the same old patterns. Why? Faulty assumptions. They think one book, workshop, or CD will set them on the right path for life. Yes, that's part of it, but not the whole answer. And, yes, it is a great start. We would like those good feelings that spark us to last. They can; it just takes time and consistent practice.

You took a shower today to wash the dirt away, and you will do it again tomorrow because you'll get dirty again. Clean your mind like you clean your body—every day. Take a motivational shower of positive thoughts, people, CDs, YouTube, music, *daily* reading, and exercise. These things are your positive bar of soap that scrubs away the negativity. You have everything to gain by keeping your thoughts and emotions "clean and dry." As Wayne Dyer said, "When you change the way you look at things, the things you look at change." And when you change the way you think about things, the things you think about change. Always remember that you are what you believe you are.

Tools

Beliefs are acquired most often through repetitive exposure to others and chanced by repetition.

- Pay attention to your thoughts and actions. Often what you don't do or won't do, tells the bigger story.
- Change your words—make them positive, especially the words about yourself.
- Listen to positive, uplifting podcasts or YouTube videos.
- Have inspiring photos where you can see them every day.
- Turn off the news (it's rarely good, and if the world is coming to an end, trust me, someone will let you know).
- Focus on a specific level of achievement, improving behaviors and processes.
- Believe you are worth it (because you are).
- Learn to control your perceptions and emotions
- Hang out with people who move you toward your goals and dreams—people who work on their own.
- Be patient.
- Practice.
- Find support and ask for help (we often need it).
- And pay attention to obstacles, don't deny them, realize they are there, and you will need to move past or through them, also known as being realistic.

Beliefs

Pay attention and change your thinking:

Old	New
If I try, make a mistake I will look dumb/stupid	Everyone makes mistakes that is how we learn, improve, and become more valuable.
All artists are poor	Many artists make an excellent living at their craft
To be a great writer you must be depressed, suffer, be alcoholic	Most writers are everyday people who love to write and are not depressed or alcoholic
All daredevils died drunk and broke	They do not have to drink and can have good final futures
You make me mad (I can make people feel)	No one can make me feel anything, I am in charge of my mind, my emotions, and actions (takes practice)
You can get polio from eating ice cream	Not true that was an actual urban myth in the 1950s
There are no good men or women out there	Not true there are many, many, good men and women, and you must be open to finding them (and working on yourself first)
It takes money to make money	Not true most people start from nothing; it does take work and time
Women are not good at math & science	Not true
Extroverts make the best salespeople	No, and there is much evidence to the contrary, introverts and extroverts both can make good salespeople

I can't change	Yes, you can, it takes a desire to change, time, practice, and support
I can't	It isn't a matter of can't, it is I haven't yet! Adapt the 'not yet' principle
I am unlovable	Yes, you are
I am not worthy	Yes, you are
Always a nice person	Being nice is good as long as aren't letting people run you over.
Better to be poor and happy (at least we are happy and are good people)	Wealthy people are happy, and they can do good things with their money. At what point do you become a bad person is it $50,000 + 1 dollar then at $50,001 you become a bad person, you change?

Chapter

4

Self-defeating Behaviors

"We have met the enemy and he is us."
~ *Pogo* by Walt Kelly, in the 1960s

We are always our own best advocate and our own worst enemy. No doubt, you've heard of STDs, ADHD, PTSD, FOMO (fear of missing out). But have you heard of the most destructive syndrome that plagues us all? SDB! Self-Defeating Behavior. No one is immune. Many of us get caught in what Scott Belsky talks about in his book, *The Messy Middle: Finding Your Way Through the Hardest and Most Crucial Part of Any Bold Adventure.* This is what I call "The Valley of Dead Dreams"—a place where most good ideas end up. Everyone experiences this—when the energy is no longer carrying you—when that initial flame becomes embers, and the ball gets dropped. (Hmm, I'm mixing metaphors.) This is when the real, hard, and sometimes boring work has begun. It is often when we get distracted by new ideas, shiny objects, doubt, fear, or just get bored. The new idea fairy comes along, and *Bing!* We are off and running toward that new thing with renewed passion, getting that dopamine pump we love so much. But what happened to the first project idea? It gets lost in the "The Valley of Dead Dreams."

Several years ago, I hired a very talented lady who said to me right off the bat, "I am not a good idea person, but I'm a great implementer." "Don't worry," I said. "I have enough ideas for five people. I just need people to help me implement them and keep moving through 'The Valley of Dead Dreams.'" And for ten years, we worked as a great team. Sadly, that collaboration ended because of her untimely death. I miss her and miss our collaboration, and our time together.

Knowing your strengths, weaknesses, or areas that need to be improved is crucial. That is where coaching and guidance come in. If you're not a good planner, find people who will help you plan. If you are a good planner but not a good implementer, find people who can implement.

What lies at the heart of our self-defeating behaviors are the lies we tell ourselves. We lie about what we think, we lie about what we want, and we lie about what we'll do to get what we want. Yup! We lie. I know because I'm a liar too. As Eric Hoffer said, "We lie loudest when we lie to ourselves." And we lie to ourselves all the time about everything—from our weight to our finances, ambitions, relationships, and what we want. We lie about everything, but mostly to ourselves.

The lies start when we are very, very young. We are brainwashed, albeit with good intentions. Here a few examples:

Be nice	And we should be as long as we aren't giving up ourselves. Some people will try to be so nice that they lose themselves.
Rich people are bad	Really? Since when? Yes, some do bad things but so do not rich people. It has little to do with wealth.
Better to be seen and not heard	Maybe that's okay when you are five and driving your parent up a wall, but really, not as an adult.
If something is meant to be, it will be	If something is meant to be, usually you need to take action—repeated action.
Anything is possible	Well, no. I am never going to sing opera, but there are other things I can do.

We've all had these experiences. What are yours? How have you been brainwashed? Explore it. These lies were often about control yet were also used to help us understand things we were too young to comprehend. Every family and culture has its lies, beliefs, and sayings.

The lies often continue as we get older yet take on a different form. We start lying to ourselves about what we feel and what we want because we were told by parents, teachers, friends, the media, and the world not to want certain things because it's not possible or they are bad. I am sure you can recall those conversations. "Do you think we're made of money?" "That's a terrible career choice." "You will never amount to anything!" "You will never be able to do that!" Blah, blah, blah.

We have to stop lying to ourselves because we cannot change anything until we stop the lies and start telling ourselves the truth. The next time you're making excuses, complaining, or blaming, *stop*! Think and ask whether you are being honest with yourself.

We aren't honest with ourselves about what we want from our lives and who we want to be. If we told the truth about what we wanted, we would need to commit to it and start working toward it. Lying allows us to remain in a state of comfort, of complacency, so we can avoid doing things that push us out of our comfort zone. We fight hard to defend our lies and excuses. We procrastinate, deny, and hide what we want and who we are. The Funny thing about the lies we tell ourselves and those others tell, it is like a conspiracy. We allow ourselves to accept others' lies, so we don't get called out on our own. I think we need to start moving toward radical but kind honesty.

When you lie to yourself about what you want, you are sabotaging yourself. Acknowledging what you want doesn't mean you have to go out and change your life today and accomplish your goals instantaneously. You define success for yourself. It simply means you need to start setting yourself up for success by doing everything we discuss in this book—paying attention, addressing your beliefs, paying attention to fear, and developing good habits by discovering what self-sabotaging behaviors you have and why.

"The truth knocks on the door, and you say, 'go away, I'm looking for the truth,' and so it goes away, puzzling."
~ Robert M. Pirsig

Opportunity paged me, beeped me, linked me, e-mailed me, faxed me, and spammed me. But I was expecting it to knock.

Understanding what you truly want can be a confusing process at times. Life is full of paradoxes. We all want to be in shape and healthy, but we most definitely want chocolate cake, too. There must be some balance, some yin and yang. If we do nothing but eat chocolate cake, we most certainly are going to die pretty quickly from obesity. However, if we do nothing but exercise, we might become bored and unmotivated. Learning to balance these paradoxes is an important life skill.

Often, our vision of what we want ultimately does come out, but if we fight it and suppress it, it may be too late. As John Greenleaf Whittier said, "For all sad words of tongue and pen, the saddest are these, 'It might have been.'"

If we don't deal with them, they can bubble to the surface and destroy our relationships, businesses, or our lives. We can become bitter. Denying the truth and lying to ourselves, which we do all too often, is not the best way to live life. We need to live in truth—our own truth about who we are and what we want.

Many of these lies stem from fear, and it is easier for us not to acknowledge the truth and cower. It's much more comfortable. But comfort is the enemy of change, joy, and success. Becoming good, then better, then great takes commitment. Comfort stops us—makes us lazy and complacent. We blame. We make excuses. We lie. And we *know* it. As Mark Twain said, "Comfort makes cowards of us all." Great quote. I love Mark Twain's writing, humor, and observations. Yet, at the same time, Twain's own self-defeating behaviors left him broke. That's right. Samuel Clemens went from being the highest-paid author of his time to losing his home.

We make up all these fantasy stories about what we're going to accomplish, and then we don't do anything about it. And the funny thing is, we could accomplish a lot with less effort than we imagine yet, we make excuses and blame. But the reality is, there are very few excuses and reasons to blame. Most of the time, the fault lies with us. Excuses and playing the blame game are huge self-defeating behaviors. Be honest with yourself and start. Any step forward is a step for the better.

Stop waiting to make your life better or for someone else to make your life better. No one is coming to rescue you. You have to make it better. If you want to lose those twenty pounds, go ahead and lose them. Do whatever it takes to reach that goal. That's how you make things happen. Again, this is where accountability, coaches, masterminds, and goal buddies are an enormous help. A mastermind is a small group of people who meet, email, and call each other regularly to support and hold each other accountable.

Self-sabotaging behavior is often associated with the belief that if everyone is doing something, then we should partake in it, too. And a piece of good advice is, don't follow the herd. We all do it. For example, many people (myself included) are guilty of going to the gym, spending an hour sweating, and then coming home and indulging in a bag of potato chips. Since obesity is a major issue in the USA and much of the world, let me pass on the words of wisdom from Scooby Werkstatt, who has a great fitness website Scooby Workouts. Scooby says, "You can't out-exercise your diet." Check out his website for useful information, videos, and calorie calculators.

How do we mitigate unhealthy behaviors that serve to limit our potential growth? By *paying attention*, examining our fears, our belief systems, and START taking action.

What baffles me, even to this day, is how often I get in my own way. How do I self-sabotage? Let me count the ways. Procrastination, lack of goals, no plan, wasting time on Facebook, and letting fear and doubt creep in. The list could go on and on. It's not just me, though. I see it all the time in my Find A Way workshops, mastermind group, and as a CFP® (Certified Financial Planner), working with clients. *You* see it all the time, too.

We see extremely successful people seemingly throw caution to the wind, jeopardizing their entire life's work on something stupid—from drugs to alcohol, gambling, cheating, lying, and taking on ridiculous risks. It's amazing how much we self-sabotage and how much self-defeating behaviors play a role in our lives.

Some of the biggest and most common forms of SDBs include procrastination, distraction, denial, making excuses, and blaming. Understand that our biggest challenge is always ourselves—the time we waste, the excuses we make, the fear we let control us. Understanding and finding a way around ourselves is the secret to getting what we want and deserve. Don't let your SDBs get in the way!

When I think about self-defeating behaviors, chicken parmesan comes to mind. Here's why. Every morning at seven o'clock, I arrive at the gym, and I see a bunch of the regulars who, amazingly, always seem to look exactly the same or have gotten even heavier over the years. Sometimes, I overhear their conversations. I understand why there seems to be little progress. They get on the exercise bikes and somehow manage to barely move. They plod along, not really putting in the effort.

Once, one of them said to the other, "Yeah, I am going out tonight for chicken parmesan," or I see them later that day eating a huge muffin.

My sense is telling me that it isn't a once-a-month special occasion. It's all the time. How else does a person end up being grossly out of shape and gaining weight when they go to the gym every day?

We screw up our lives 90% of the time. In the documentary *People vs. the State of Illusion*, it is estimated that 50% of deaths in the United States each year are attributable to behavioral or social factors. These are deaths from preventable factors such as over-eating, not exercising and ignoring our physical and mental health in general, excess drinking, drugs, drinking and driving, smoking—all the things we shouldn't be doing. All these behaviors are *choices* that *we make every day.* Yes, SDBs are something we actually *practice* every day.

> "Never put off 'til tomorrow what you can do the day after tomorrow just as well."
> ~ Mark Twain

How Self-Critical Are You?

For each of the following statements, indicate the number that best describes how you feel most of the time.

Totally disagree; 2. Disagree very much; 3. Disagree slightly; 4. Neutral; 5. Agree slightly; 6. Agree very much; 7. Totally agree

___1. It is difficult to be happy unless one is good-looking, intelligent, rich, and creative.

___2. People will probably think less of me if I make a mistake.

___3. If I do not do well all the time, people will not respect me.

___4. If I ask for help, it is a sign of weakness.

___5. If I do not do as well as other people, it means I am a weak person.

___6. If I fail at my work, then I am a failure as a person.

___7. If I cannot do something well, there is little point in doing it at all.

___8. If someone disagrees with me, it probably indicates he does not like me.

___9. If I fail partly, it is as bad as being a complete failure.

___10. If other people know what I am really like, they will think less of me.

___11. If I don't set the highest standards for myself, I am likely to end up a second-rate person.

___12. If I am to be a worthwhile person, I must be the best in at least one way.

___13. People who have good ideas are better than those who do not.

___14. I should be upset if I make a mistake.

___15. If I ask a question, it makes me look stupid.

A total score of 54 and above indicates a high level of self-criticism and perfectionism, 39 is average, and 24 or less represents a low level.

Source: Dysfunctional Attitude Scale by Weissman, A.N. & Beck, A.T., 1978; Imber et al., 1990

Self-defeating Behaviors

There is one self-defeating behavior that's so big I wanted to start a support group for it. It's called Procrastinators Anonymous (PA). Problem is, I never got around to organizing it. If the "pro-" in procrastination stands for professional, then I might be the pro-procrastinator. Unfortunately, procrastinating is not a highly sought-after skill. In fact, it's very costly.

I can't begin to tell you how many times I have procrastinated on booking a room or a plane flight only to find out it was sold out or the price jumped. And it's not like it was such a difficult task to accomplish.

In the article, *New Perspectives on Procrastination* (Frontiers Media SA), procrastination is described as "the voluntary delay of an intended course of action despite expecting to be worse off because of the delay." Put another way, you already know what to do, but you're not doing it. Basically, you are screwing yourself. This is where you need to Suck It Up, Cupcake, and *stop*! Many of us choose not to act until the consequences and fear of inaction exceed the fear of doing. Sometimes it happens too late. Here is a perfect example of what I mean.

I once owned a pop-up camping trailer that the kids and I used all the time when they were young, though less and less (zero, actually) once they got older. But I was convinced that I would still use it. I was offered $1,400 for it (and that was back in the day when $1,400 would go a bit farther), but I turned it down because I was so certain I would use it. Then a few years later, I got an offer for $500, then $300. But again, I said, "No." I never did use it. Well, I am sure you guessed it by now. I never did sell it. I ended up paying someone $200 to tow it away years later.

What a huge loss! What was I thinking? Or maybe, what wasn't I thinking? First, I wasn't realistic. Clearly, using that trailer wasn't a top priority of mine, and the motivation wasn't there. Second, I procrastinated on such a little thing!

How hard would it have been just to accept the money? In fact, just as an aside, had I accepted the $1,400 and invested it, today it could be worth about $5,600, plus the $200 I paid to have it towed.

Yet, I still procrastinate, even on the smallest and dumbest things. And procrastinating would make my life simpler and less chaotic. In the long run, I would feel better and have more time for other things.

What about you? Don't be your own worst enemy.

The burning question, as always, is why? Why do I procrastinate? Why do you? Are we afraid to move to the next level? Are we afraid of not fitting in? Maybe we are too afraid to pay the price, so we acquiesce or maybe believe we have more time than we do.

Even at my age, which is seven decades, I still don't know where I fit in. To be honest, I feel like I should know the answers to these questions by now. I wrote my last book in 2009, and it has taken me over ten years to write and publish this book. If I had written one page per week, I would have had about a fifty-two-page book by the end of the year—in four years, 208 pages. So why has it taken me over a decade? It isn't that I haven't been writing or doing research. I have every day. But I allowed the small stuff to get in the way. Oh, yes, I had plenty of excuses . . . I mean reasons. How should I begin the book? Should I start with a great quote, a story, or humor? Eventually, I made it a priority, stopped making excuses, and asked myself, "What do I want you to know?" What do you want to know as a reader? From there, I just stopped procrastinating and started writing.

Procrastination is a killer. It kills our dreams, our potential, and our gifts and can physically kill us. We are experts in justifying our excuses and developing convincing arguments for why we didn't just get it done. Most of us are "Excuse Masters."

So, what causes it? It's a multitude of factors: fear, the perception that we have time later, the belief that what we want to do now is better or more important. Or we aren't ready. And here is a tip; *rarely are we ready or feel like it's the right time.* This is where we need to understand a little bit about our brains. It's lazy! It doesn't like discomfort (change, fear), so it will talk us out of everything every time. It is human nature to try and find the easiest possible way, the safest, most comfortable way. But often, that means not doing anything. The difference between a successful person and a not-so-successful one is that the successful person finds ways to push through the discomfort and procrastination. They Suck It Up.

"Procrastination is my sin; brings me constant sorrow. I really shouldn't practice it; perhaps I'll stop tomorrow."
~ J.K. Lasser

I hope none of you will have this sorrow. Please don't wake up one day and realize you could have been so much more because the regret you feel will be debilitating when you realize that it's your fault. Remember; discipline is light, regret is heavy.

Tony Robbins said, "The road to someday leads to a town called Nowhere." And let me tell you, I bet that's where the gods of distraction live. Remember, "Someday" is not a day of the week, and neither is "one day." Yet the more we procrastinate, the more we become a procrastinator. It's a compound effect. It's easier to continue procrastinating once you start.

Start by asking yourself, "What am I waiting for?" Are you waiting for the right place or the right time? Are you waiting to feel ready? What, exactly, are you insisting will happen before you start selling your art, writing that book, building that house, taking that hike, hiring a coach? Write down what you believe must happen in order to start and why you believe it has to happen. Being clear about what you're waiting for, about what is standing in your way, enables you to make the changes necessary for progress and success.

Life is long, longer than we like to believe. Yes, life *is not* short; we just waste much of it. As you make changes and take more time to get the things that will move you forward done, others may not always understand. A word of advice: it's okay to be selfish with your time, to allow time for getting things done, as long as you are not ignoring the people in your life who matter. Always remember to be selfish with your time and kind to people.

Excuses/Blaming/Responsibility

"If it is important to you, you'll make the time. If not, you'll make an excuse."
~ Marie Forleo

Excuses and blame are part of a huge epidemic, a conspiracy. It is a conspiracy because we make excuses, and no one calls us on them. So, we don't call them on their excuses. If you are honest with yourself—like cross-my-heart-and-hope-to-die honest—what's one area where if you stopped making sorry-ass excuses, you could totally turn the beat around on your life? What specific excuse do you need to drop like a hot potato?

Self-defeating Behaviors

Drop excuses like a hot potato

Excuses I need to drop

We all make excuses—tons of them. One I've heard too often is, "I've got a life. It can't be all about work." While that's absolutely true, it doesn't mean we can use it as an excuse not to get our work done. Think about this. Two generations ago, people used to work six-to-seven days a week for ten-to-twelve hours every day (averaging 2,800 hours per year) just to *survive* and provide for their families. Most of us don't have to do that now. I think it's crap that we make up excuses just to avoid putting in a little extra work. As my friend Charlie Cook, says, "Stop looking for an excuse like there is a reward," because the reward comes from putting in the extra time and work to reach your goals, not the other way around.

Priorities

Have you ever said something like, "I wish I had more money," "I wish I were in better shape," or "I wish I (you fill in the blank)?" If you haven't made progress in your journey to fulfilling that wish, you are lying to yourself about how much you want it. It's a lie because if you really wanted to, you could have done it. You can lose weight, earn that extra money, and have a better life if you stopped wishful thinking, made your goals a priority, and took action.

The truth is, we always do what we want to do. People think they're out of control, but we are all in control of our lives. And we do exactly what we want to do even though we may not think we do. You are doing it right now, and so am I. Unfortunately for some, doing what you want means doing nothing.

Too often, we blame circumstances or blame people. We blame all types of things. But once we hit a certain point in our lives, we are in charge. You're reading this right now because you have chosen to do so. You always have a choice. Even if sometimes you don't like the options, it's still a choice. You are in control and you are responsible.

Ralph Waldo Emerson's *The Essay on Self-Reliance* should be required reading for everyone. We need to start taking responsibility for ourselves . . . period.

We point our fingers, blame, and complain, but we don't want to do anything about it. We are the problem. Just remember the saying: when you point your finger of blame, three fingers are pointing back at you. Every one of us has done this at some point. We don't take care of our health, families, and finances, then we try to dump it all onto a system that will eventually collapse under its own weight. If we want to make America great, we need to start taking personal responsibility for everything in our lives and encourage others to do the same. Guide them. Help them.

Help them in a way that will set them free, not keep them prisoners of themselves or the system.

Whether it's your health, finances, or relationships, as soon as you have an inkling about what you want to do, in comes the "No." No money, no time, no experience, no degree, and then the *numero uno* excuse; "I can't." I am a firm believer that we, that is, you and me, can do almost anything we want. But when we make excuses, we disempower ourselves and our mind turns away from the goals and moves toward excuses. Eventually, we begin to believe that we actually "can't" and will look for the reasons we can't. Again, that is called confirmation bias—seeking and assigning more weight to evidence that confirms one's beliefs, while at the same time, ignoring evidence that could disaffirm their belief. We forget that we are the ones who decided we couldn't in the first place.

That is when we must pay attention to fear and seek counsel from a mentor, coach, or goal buddy. Find ways to build accountability in your life. This isn't new thinking. "Even hungry cattle in sight of pasture need the prod," Heraclitus wrote in 500 BC. So, when people say things are different today or were easier in the old days, they are full of crap. That is an excuse . . . period.

We let fear override and overrun us, so we distract ourselves. But whatever we run away from, we will eventually run into. When we run, we don't only run away from responsibility, but we also are running away from our potential, our dreams, and the possibility of a great life in favor of one average or less than average. Ask yourself, "Am I not paying attention, or do I not care enough?"

Often, the things we give up, like our goals, we are giving up for our distractions. We waste time, and what happens? We give up on the greater good for a much lesser good—really a bunch of junk. Distractions can be fun. Trust me; I get it. I'm not against fun in any shape or form. But when fun and distractions get in the way of our true goals, it becomes a whole other issue.

Distraction Vampires

Let's consider distractions. I believe that most of us can do almost anything if we want it enough. But too many of us let our distractions get in our way—like vampires sucking up our time and energy. Here's a personal example. Earlier I lost, yes lost, thirty minutes wasting time watching scenes from *Police Academy* on YouTube. Yup! Thirty minutes wasted . . . gone.

See what I mean? And it happens to us way too often; this is part of the lie we tell ourselves. The result? We become lazy and unfocused. We need to pay attention to how we focus our time and energy. Yet, we tend to spend so much of our time listening to the news and focusing our energy on the daily lives, successes, failures, and idiosyncrasies of others—again, mostly a bunch of crap. Who really cares if a movie star forgot to brush his teeth or wore an ugly suit? Who cares if that basketball player missed a shot? We scrutinize and pry into the lives of people who have little or no significance in our daily lives when we could be using that time and energy to focus on digging deeper into our own lives. Of course, this is scary. We need to remove the constant static from our lives and use the time to work on ourselves, and our goals.

We are drunk on our distractions, and most of us are still drinking because we are addicted. Well, I can guarantee you a hangover is coming. In ten or twenty years, you'll wake up and wonder what you did with your life. We all need to detox from useless distractions.

There is a belief that all our energy and power are locked up in our addictions. And once we kill those addictions, we get all our energy and power back. Addictions are our distractions, and they rob us of our potential, our life, our greatness, and our goodness. They rob us of the life we're meant to live, stealing our precious, valuable time.

Distractions come in many different forms, and we aren't even aware of them. Removing or even minimizing distractions leads to an increase in productivity and progress. Small changes count. I am not implying that you should cast aside your family, friends, and all fun activities. Just consider if what you are doing brings value to your life. We need to remove distractions, like the television, Facebook, and games involving Pokémon or Angry Birds that do not serve a useful purpose in our lives. If Facebook truly adds value to your life, that's okay, but schedule it into your fun time, not your work time. If most people worked just five more hours a week on something worthwhile, they would be amazed at how their life changed.

You need to focus on what will move you in the direction you most want to go. And not just at this moment, but in the future—a year, two, or five years from now.

Choose how you use your time wisely and avoid wasting time on trivial things that don't add value. You don't need to become a workaholic or let your relationships take the backseat. Well, you might need to sometimes for short periods, but you need to carefully choose what is important to you and focus on your top priorities.

We waste so much time keeping busy (and doing less work), and at the end of the day, we wonder what the heck happened to the day? There goes another day without accomplishing anything. And it sucks up even more of our motivation as we realize we are no closer to reaching our goals. Our distractions are a dangerously deceptive saboteur of our goals.

It all comes down to developing discipline and continuing to be motivated to reach your goals. Stop majoring in the minor things and focus on the major things— you, your potential, and what you really want.

I love television, and I work very hard to avoid watching commercials, the news, or just too much TV in general. Especially commercials full of actors playing games on their phones or the latest app, showing different ways you can sabotage your success. One reason many people are only dreaming about a great life is that they are watching stupid stuff on TV or their computer (guilty as charged) instead of things that will move them toward their goals. Shut off the screens and work on you.

Get Off the Pity Pot (and Make Sure You Stay Off)

What keeps you from living life to its fullest? Anxiety? A dead-end job? Depression? Anger? Chronic health problems? Feelings of inferiority? Memories of an unhappy childhood or guilt over past mistakes that you can't seem to shake? If you are caught up with these questions, you may discover a dozen scenarios that make them seem out of your control. Some of them certainly are to a degree, but we all make choices about how we handle them.

Complaining and whining are toxic and keep us down, disempowering us. It might feel good at the moment because complaining and whining allow you to let yourself off the hook. Stop complaining, stop whining, and stop screwing yourself.

Stop those SDBs! Start to get more of the life you want. When you acknowledge that everything is your choice, the realization is frightening, it sucks, yet it is empowering, too. Start *now*!

Steps to Take Now

- Most importantly, *never* beat yourself up! Ever!
- Schedules and plans are not a prison. They are paths. And, yes, you can schedule time for fun.
- Schedule appointments for activities (with someone else, so you have to show up).
- Make the next appointment while you are there.
- Get an accountability partner. (More on this in chapter seven)
- Make the invisible visible. (Put things in your way so you can't miss them)
- Set aside a time and place each day to work on yourself and what you want. You may have to start skipping the lunchroom or water cooler. Others may comment, but remember, it's your life!
- Be patient yet persistent.
- Make behavior contracts with an accountability partner. I usually recommend a $500 penalty. (More in chapter seven.)

Here are some tools and ideas that may help:

- **Clarity** is crucial. It is much harder to work on unclear, fuzzy goals and objectives. Clarity gives you a concrete place to start, steps, and a path to follow. For example, Today I will by 4:00 P.M. Set a clear timeline, such as:

    o I need this done in two weeks. I will work on it for thirty minutes each day during my lunch break or before I come into the office.
    o What do I need to accomplish each day? Break the goal into small, incremental steps.

This will get the job done, give you less stress, and often more free time.

- **Create steps** to go with your plan. If there isn't a plan and steps, it's too easy to get overwhelmed. What happens then? We freeze, and nothing happens.

- **Incentives** Here is where I often fall down. I don't give myself little incentives or rewards. When I don't, my brain says, "Screw you. I am not doing this. You always cheat me out of the reward, so no dice, buddy." Remember: set small objectives and give yourself small internal rewards sprinkled with a few small external rewards. This is actual brain science, aka neuroscience. Check out some of the work by Andrew Huberman, Ph.D., Stanford University on YouTube.

Lack of clarity results in little getting created. My friend, Brian, says, "I like confusion. It is my scapegoat. If I don't have clear goals, I don't fail. Of course, I don't succeed, either."

LIST SDBs

Which self-defeating behaviors do you use most? Pick your top three and write them on a piece of paper. Now pick your top three from the list below that you want to work on first. List some small steps you could take.

Examples: *I will set aside ten minutes each day at break time to read something that will improve my performance. I will write as much as I can. I will get fresh air and walk.*

Self-Defeating Behaviors

Abrasiveness	Having unrealistic expectations
Abrasive Behavior	Inferiority
Anger or hostility	Isolation
Binging	Negativity
Comparing yourself to others and always coming up short	Not exercising- inactivity
Complaining	Overeating
Controlling	Perfectionism
Criticizing	Procrastination
Defensiveness	Rigidity
Dependence on alcohol or antidepressants to	Self-centeredness

deal with normal daily stress	
Depression	Shyness
Eating the wrong foods or overeating	Smoking
Focusing on your appearance rather than the person you are inside	Suspiciousness
Not following up	Watching too much TV
Not asking (for help, etc.)	Worrying
Taking on too much, so you automatically fail (grandiosity)	Others:
No plan or steps	Unrealistic expectations
No boundaries	Priorities/schedule (or if everything is a priority, then nothing is)
Worrying too much about WOPT (What other people think)	Being nice, no matter what. I need to be agreeable and nice.

You know what to do to take care of yourself, so get started. Remember: a schedule is not a prison, it is a path, and structure gives you freedom.

Tools

1. Exercise fills your brain with oxygen and serotonin.
2. Focus on better nutrition. Eat healthier food.
3. Water is vital.
4. Work on a plan to help yourself from feeling overwhelmed.
5. Take a nature walk. It's a great way to revitalize.
6. It's all about mindset, and your thoughts. Pay attention.
7. Meditate, pray, walk in nature, or listen to good, positive music, CD, YouTube videos, or read. Whatever works for you.
8. Get a coach, mentor, or mastermind group. Talk to a friend or get a goal buddy.
9. Don't get stuck on the pity pot rehashing everything over and over. Once it's over, it's over. Debrief, learn the lesson, and move on.
10. Be kind to yourself. Do not beat yourself up, and don't let yourself off the hook.
11. Learn to pay attention and be *grateful* for what you have. We all forget to do this, and it is important.
12. Set up hard target dates and find ways to be held accountable.

Here's the bottom line. No one is coming to rescue you. There is no Tooth Fairy, Santa Claus, or magic. It is up to you. It always has been and always will be up to you. So, Suck It Up, Cupcake!

I want to repeat this. Never beat yourself up!
If beating yourself up actually worked, you'd be perfect by now.

Pay Attention and Be Self-aware

"One afternoon a sage monk is walking in the garden and he looks at his reflection in the water of a small calm pool. Observing his reflection, he contemplates. In the shadows is a young monk thinking he has caught his master in an act of vanity. He approaches his master and says, "Master, I see you gazing at your reflection in the water." To which the master replies, "Yes, I am. I do so to remind myself that I am both the source and solution to all my problems."

~ Zen Tales

Creating joy, health, and success—financial and otherwise— is not rocket science. It is easier than you might imagine if you pay attention, develop yourself, develop clear values and goals, make a plan, and follow it. Oh, and ask for help and guidance when you need it, even when you think you don't. I became interested in behavior and motivation many years ago when I read Dr. Norman Vincent Peale's book, *The Power of Positive Thinking.* That book poured gasoline on a small fire, igniting my interest.

I began to wonder what made me do what I did and think what I thought? By simply questioning myself, I began to become more aware of not only myself, but of others. When I started in sales, I knew I had to pay attention to human behavior. As I slowly practiced observing others, I became fascinated, and the questions kept coming: What makes us tick? Why are some people happy and others not? Why do so many people settle? Why do people squander their gifts, talents, or potential? Why do some people know more about the football standings than their own financial standing? I became interested in why people take jobs they don't like or stay in relationships that make them unhappy. Why are some of us successful and others are not?

I was always very curious about people and about myself. I enjoyed listening to lectures and learning, but I guess school just didn't float my boat. I think maybe if I had hunkered down, I would have stayed in school. Back in high school, I remember observing kids who I thought were super smart yet seemed to waste so much time—constantly struggling and getting in their own way. What I came to realize was that I was beginning to understand myself, my style, and what might work for me. Over the years, some of the other kids, the ones who were not considered smart, who were the wise guys or troublemakers, thrived. Many of them started businesses and had successful careers. They, like me, were not defined by the system.

That came to light when I decided to become a Certified Financial Planner®. I had to bury my head in the books, and suddenly, I was able to do it. What happened? For starters, I was pursuing something that *interested me, something I really wanted,* and I found my way of doing it. I discovered the power of *want* and that I love to learn, but I didn't love having to study what others wanted me to study. I loved to learn and study what I wanted to because it was of value to me. What I studied increased my knowledge and value. I started paying attention, and I came to realize that what was important was learning—gaining valuable information. And I had to change the way I thought about studying and what interested me.

If you are not paying attention to what you want, you will miss opportunities. Opportunities are everywhere, yet most people never see them because they aren't paying attention. Paying attention means getting crystal clear about what you want and what works best for you, your goals, circumstances, and your environment. Oh, and the sooner you get this, the better.

> "Men and women are anxious to improve their circumstances but are unwilling to improve themselves; they, therefore, remain bound. The person who does not shrink from self-crucifixion can never fail to accomplish the object upon which their heart is set. This is as true of earthly as of heavenly things. Even the individuals whose sole object is to acquire wealth must be prepared to make great personal sacrifices before they can accomplish their objective; and how much more so they who would realize a strong well poised life?"
>
> ~ James Allen, *As a Man Thinketh* (1903)

James Allen uses the term self-crucifixion as a metaphor for self-knowledge, accepting the imperfect and working around them. That's a point made by all great philosophers. Even the great philosopher Clint Eastwood, in the movie *Magnum Force*, said, "A man's got to know his limitations."

Pay Attention and Be Self-aware

Knowing yourself and your limitations is not about beating yourself up or taking away from your potential. It is about facing the fact we all have limitations. We need to know what they are and find ways around them.

We all have to do things we don't like sometimes. It's part of life. The secret is to look for things we do like and work toward them as much as possible. It's all about our state of mind; it is all up to you. To figure it out, we need to start paying attention, be curious about ourselves and discover what works for us.

Curiosity is an important human trait because it helps override fears and drives engagement. When your engagement increases, so does personal satisfaction and productivity. By paying attention and being curious, you not only learn about yourself, but you improve your ability to listen deeply to others and develop a sense of intuitiveness and empathy.

Through my analysis of human behavior, I began to learn more about what holds us back and how our thoughts create our actions and silently shape our lives. If they aren't the right thoughts, there won't be the right actions, and you can become your own worst enemy.

Socrates said, "The unexamined life is not worth living." Without examining and understanding yourself, you cannot grow. You must be aware of not only your own life but of those around you and the opportunities that may present themselves. I am reminded of this every day when I am driving. I pay attention to other drivers, and when I see someone waiting to turn or exit a side street, I give them that opportunity. But all too often, they aren't even paying attention! They are playing on their phones or talking to someone. Well, guess what? I can't wait around all day for them to go, so they miss their opportunity. Pay attention, careful attention, so as not to miss an opportunity when it appears.

It happens all the time in life. If you don't pay attention and take action, you might miss opportunities because they can come and go quickly. Let this serve as a small reminder to be aware and pay attention when and an opportunity presents itself. This, too, is why clear intentions, objectives, and goals are important—they help us focus and pay attention.

Sometimes, however, you need to make others pay attention to you. If no one is presenting you with the opportunity, start edging up there cautiously, and take some action. Make them notice until the opportunity arises. Then go!

Pay Attention to Your Thoughts

Many people go through life willy-nilly, not realizing that they are simply playing the programs that have been installed. Most of our programing happened during the early stages of our lives. Depending on what was installed and is now playing, those old programs have a huge impact on the direction of our lives. Even if some programs are not helpful, we keep on playing them over and over until we pay attention to them.

We live each day according to our internal scripts, and we let the voices in our head, the silent "voices" known only through our actions or feelings, decide what we can and can't do, what we deserve or don't deserve, and what heights we can or cannot reach. The reality is that you need to choose what plays in your head, and only you can filter these messages through awareness by paying attention. As I like to say, "You can't repair if you're not aware."

Pay attention to your thoughts, especially when thinking about your goals and accomplishing your dreams. Do you say "I can," or are you impeded by such thoughts as "I can't" or "No one can." Your negative self-talk sparks self-doubt and it shuts off your creative ability.

When you think of the infamous "I can't," your mind immediately looks for all the reasons why you can't instead of working through how you can. When you think "I can," your mind begins to find all the ways you can. As long as you hold that *can-do* thought and focus, your mind will continue to find ways to make it happen. Your mind is a goal-achieving machine if you pay attention, feed it the right material, and keep it oiled. Tell yourself, "I will be open to ideas and opportunities." Always remember, your mind will work in the direction you focus on either "I can't" or "I can."

Combined with paying attention to how you talk to yourself, also pay attention to:

1. what you are reading or listening to
2. who you associate with
3. how you feel
4. where you are working or hanging out. Your environment is critical
5. what you are *not* doing

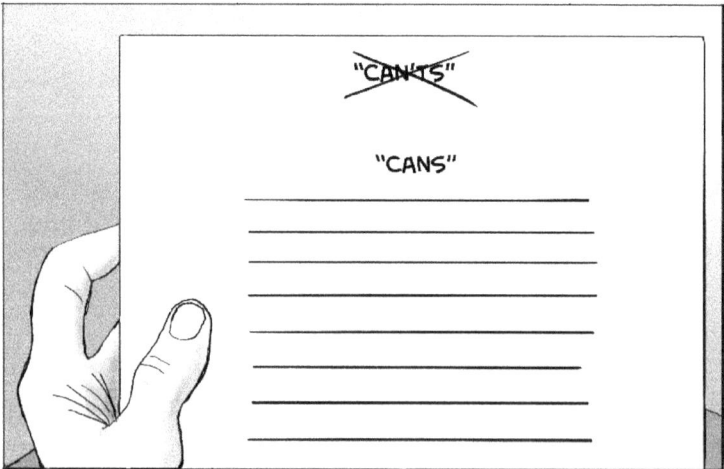

Take a piece of paper and at the top write something you would like to accomplish. On the left side, under what you would like to accomplish, write **Can't**, and on the right side, write **Can**. Now start to write—first on the left and then on the right.

By making this list, did you notice a difference? A change in thinking? A change in feeling? You may have had feelings of doubt and fear, but did you notice a change in your confidence, and your ability to do things differently? Let your mind work on the Can for the next few days— maybe a week. Every time you think of a Can, add it to your list. Notice how your mind will begin to search for ways to help you. It does, and it will, as long as you allow it to. Be aware that along with the positive I Cans, fear and doubt will attempt to crash your party. Notice these and let them go!

Keep writing. As an aside, make sure you always have a way to jot down your thoughts, always have paper and pen, and use your phone or Post-it notes. I even have erasable markers in my shower so I can write things on the shower wall before I froget. The funny thing about good ideas is they can come and go quickly, so we need to capture them immediately.

The great part about the scripts in your head is that you can rewrite them at any time if you are so inclined. You decide how you want to talk to yourself, so start allowing positive messages to play in your head. You can choose your beliefs and the way you want to be, and what you want to do with your life.

Pay attention to your thoughts, especially to your yeah but thoughts and your judgments. There is no such thing as being nonjudgmental. We judge everything. Most important is how you judge yourself. (That is the hard stuff.)

Stop telling yourself things that make you weak. It's your job to deprogram the messages you send yourself—that don't work and are not serving you. That requires effort and, of course, time, patience, and attention. This new way of attending to your thoughts will ripple through your entire life. As you get better, everyone and everything around you gets better.

Pay Attention to Your Actions

Not only should you pay attention to your thoughts, pay close attention to your actions. What you say and what you do are often two different things. Words are powerful, and what you actually *do* is even more powerful. Remember the adage, "Actions speak louder than words." Learn to pay attention to your words, what you do, and even more importantly, what you *don't do*.

If you say you want to accomplish something specific and then don't follow through, the tendency is to ignore it. When you fail to take action, or if your actions are contrary or inconsistent with what you say, you need to pay close attention to determine what's going on and why. This helps you learn about yourself.

When you fail to do something you said you were going to do, stop and think, "Did I truly mean I wanted to" (fill in the blank) _____? "Or am I just fooling myself? Was I engaged in wishful thinking, or is something getting in my way? Could it be fear? A poor or bad script (belief) playing, such as I failed at this before, so why try it again?' or 'I don't have the skills or talent, so why bother?"

Introspection can be challenging, even painful, but it is very important. As Jack Nicholson said in the movie, *A Few Good Men*, "You can't handle the truth!" But you need to. You need to be crystal clear with yourself.

And always, always remember that this self-aware practice is never about feeling bad about yourself or beating yourself up. It is about being true to who you are, who you are meant to be, and what you are meant to do with your life.

106

The first step in designing your life your way is self-awareness. When we pay attention, everything in our life improves. I remind people of this at my Firewalking seminars. The more you pay attention to your health, the more your health improves. The same goes for relationships, your career, and your finances. It all gets better when you pay attention. Let me repeat: you can't repair if you are not aware!

"The innermost in due time becomes the outermost, which means life is an inside game. In other words, fix your inside first, set your beliefs and your goals, and the rest will follow."
~ Ralph Waldo Emerson

Life is lived from the inside out and not the outside in. We focus so much on the outside part because it's what we and others see and what the media tell us or brainwash us with. It is what's on the inside that shapes our life on the outside. It is learning about our insides, our inner self—how we talk to ourselves, react to situations, and handle issues—that allows us to move forward. This is the part of us that requires most of our attention and is crucial to our development. Your life, business, career, relationships, everything, is a direct reflection of your inner self. This is why paying attention is so important.

Never Try to Put a Square Peg in a Round Hole

You may have heard the adage, "Never try to put a square peg in a round hole." The reason should obvious. It won't fit. The goal needs to be to find what fits you.

We are supposed to work at making life simpler, not harder. I am not saying we don't have to work hard and struggle sometimes, but we also have to be logical about it. When we try to fit in the wrong hole, we are simply getting in our own way and wasting time and our lives. Knowing which type of peg will make our lives easier. I am not saying that there aren't times when we have to be flexible and adapt. Of course, there are.

Be aware, pay attention, and make sure your life, career, and relationships fit you.

For example, talking with people comes easy to me. I'm not saying I don't have to work at it sometimes because I do. But overall, it's something that comes naturally to me. Now, if you put a hammer in my hand, there would be conflict brewing unless it was to tear something down. I could learn carpentry or computer programing or something that didn't fit my strengths or temperament. But it might be difficult and a waste of effort.

My suggestion is to find what fits you and get really good at it. You can learn almost any skill and do it well. If it's always an uphill battle because it is a poor fit, you may become miserable. It doesn't matter what talents or skills you have. What matters are the talents and skills you have that you use. The world is full of talented, skilled people who never share their gifts. You have to learn and understand yourself by finding your strengths and weaknesses. Then capitalize on the strengths you discover and find ways around your weaknesses to minimize their impact.

I'm wealthy beyond my wildest dreams! Unfortunately, my dreams were never very wild.

Pay attention to the things you are drawn to—that you have a knack for doing. Ask yourself these questions and make a list:

- What comes easier to me?
- What do I enjoy?
- Which abilities can I use or develop?
- Where could those abilities be applied?
- Who would pay me for the skills I have or can develop?

If you aren't sure about your strengths, you could ask friends what they see are your strengths and potential; just be ready for the answers.

Sometimes, we don't pay attention to what comes easy to us. We take our skills for granted and may even assume everyone else can do the same. No! Not everyone has your skills, talents, and training. Don't *assume*.

Discovering yourself is a lifelong journey. Learn to enjoy it. Life isn't perfect. Even if you have the best career, relationship, or plan, there are always a few bumps along the road. You just need to keep in mind, "This too shall pass," and be as true to yourself as you can.

You can be successful in almost any career path. You can develop a process to become wealthy if that is what you want. You have to have a plan, a system, and follow through. Paying attention and knowing yourself is the first step on the true path to prosperity and happiness. So, stop reading and get practicing! (Well, stop reading for now and then come back and finish this book!)

Take Action NOW

GOLDEN TRIANGLE

Tools

- You can't repair if you are not aware. Record your thoughts and ideas, even if you don't use them immediately.

- Always have a pen and paper or recording device handy. Send yourself emails or texts of your ideas or insights.
- Incorporate meditation, walking, weeding the garden, or some peaceful thinking time into your daily routine.
- Give yourself permission to want what you want and do what you want.
- Be grateful. Keep a daily gratitude journal.
- Invest in you, time, energy, and money.
- There are many websites that have assessment tools to help you get clear on your strengths

  o www.gallup.com
  o Meyers Briggs (just Google, also there are many great YouTube videos)

6

Compound Effect

We've all heard about the power of compound interest when we talk about money in the bank or investments. Yet, we don't think about the power of compounding in our daily lives. Compounding is a powerful concept in all aspects of our lives, not just our finances. *Everything* we do or don't do, adds up and moves us toward our goals or away from them. Albert Einstein once called compound interest the Eighth Wonder of the World. I believe *"Compound Effort"* is the ninth. Do not discount this effect or *its power*. It is easy to do because it is so subtle it often goes unnoticed.

Our actions, thoughts, and behaviors are always compounding. You can't go to the gym once and expect to look like Arnold Schwarzenegger (not that you want to look like Arnold, but you catch my drift). A buff body requires compounding—repetitive and consistent action. The same applies to your investments, health, career, relationships, and life. Not going to the gym or exercising is also compounding, just in the wrong direction.

All things in life are subject to the compound effect. Even the smallest things can make an enormous difference. If you drank one less can of Coke a day, that's 365 Cokes per year. You would have saved yourself 51,100 calories and 14,235 grams of sugar on top of saving some money and improving your health. That adds up. Now imagine that for five to ten years! Imagine if you walked an extra ten minutes per day in your lifetime. As the old saying goes, life is not a hundred-yard dash, it's a marathon; every step counts up.

Understanding this principle but failing to apply it can wreak havoc on your life. Understanding the compound effect and applying it can create health, happiness, and even wealth. So, let's start by *paying attention*. Pay attention to all the choices you make every day because each is a steppingstone on your journey. Each choice creates an effect, and they all combine and compound over time. Most of them are so small and subtle that we don't give much thought to how they will play into the big picture.

If you gave someone a hug today or smiled, or said something nice, would it change the world? You know what? It could. It could change your life and theirs, that day, and perhaps even forever. Yet, we don't pay attention or stop to think how powerful small actions can be. Let's break it down. Suppose you smiled at someone, said hello, and complimented them. They feel better and will most likely do the same to another person who then does or says something nice to someone else. One nice gesture can start a forward process that could make the world better, even if only for a moment. A wonderful example of this type of thinking was powerfully illustrated several years ago in the movie *Pay It Forward*.

Compound Effect is Habit

I was about thirty-five when I began getting up early in the morning. I would hop out of bed and zip down to the coffee shop to meet my business partner. We were building houses together and had to meet before we both went to our regular day jobs. Dave was a carpenter; I had my insurance and real estate businesses. That first, fresh, hot cup of coffee, its aroma . . . that's what got me charged, and I could quickly jump into my work. That was when I discovered that I could accomplish a lot first thing in the morning.

I continued to get up bright and early and use that time to study for my CFP® and my Series 7 Securities License (a Series 7 is a stockbroker's license) and later to write. Each of those things increased my value as a businessperson. By 5:30 a.m., you could find me with a hot cup of joe glued to my seat for two hours. I studied that way for two years, plus extra time during the evenings and on Saturdays and Sundays. The only day I skipped was Christmas Day.

As time passed and I accomplished many goals, I would move from one to the next. I wrote my first book, my second book, and this one using this exact same method. I blocked off the time, jumped out of bed early, read, researched, and wrote. Although each project was different, the technique I used had not changed. I found my peak performance time, structured my environment, and got into a great new habit that has compounded. And I protect it. On the rare occasion when I get detoured, I don't beat myself up. I just go back the next morning. I had found what Hal Elrod wrote about in his 2012 book, *The Miracle Morning*, but twenty years earlier!

I continue to carve out the time and space to work on my goals. And I don't let others interfere unless it's for a coffee refill, of course. Protect your time. As each morning (or evening if you are a night person) compounds, you'll grow and develop. When thinking about the compound effect, some people might think small changes won't work. Oh really? Then remember this: little hinges swing big doors.

Early mornings in the coffee shop became my routine. Habits are one of the best examples of the compound effect; they create the world we inhabit. Our habits are invisible decisions that we have already made. We all have habits, but we don't pay attention to them. Some of our habits serve you well, such as wearing your seatbelt, locking your door, putting your keys in the same place, and brushing your teeth.

On the other hand, many habits can be destructive, leading to self-defeating behaviors and patterns. Here are a few examples:

- over-eating
- not exercising
- letting yourself become a victim
- whining
- blaming
- making excuses
- complaining (I was good at this)
- sloppy work
- procrastination
- ignoring relationships
- ignoring reality
- not planning for future
- not developing yourself

There also are instances of valuable compounding positive behaviors:

- exercising, walking, weightlifting (at any age)
- learning to relax-breathe-meditate, walk—whatever works for you

- taking responsibility, no blaming or complaining (at least complaining less, lol)
- giving hugs
- building accountability
- paying attention (mindfulness)
- making plans, hiring a coach, finding a goal buddy
- having a schedule is one of your best tools

It's difficult, yet critical, to examine your behaviors, understand where they come from, and decide which ones are helping you. Stick with the habits that serve you and swap them out for those that create havoc and chaos in your life—the ones that stop you from achieving your dreams.

The next step is to build habits congruent with the life you want to live. Conditions don't determine your destiny; your character does. Your habits shape your character. If you want to learn how to be successful, begin by replacing your bad habits with good ones. It will take some time, so it's best not to overwhelm yourself. Most habits are created slowly over time.

Making habits that are easy to adopt and *sustainable* is key to becoming more successful in your endeavors to create anything. Too often, people jump into huge commitments, then nothing comes of them, mostly because they have no behaviors to support the plan. So, they abandon such changes because they are too large and unsustainable.

Another way we can get caught up in the "The Valley of Dead Dreams" is by buying into what I call the "Uncle Willie Effect." Most people have an Uncle Willie—the guy who drank excessively, smoked two packs of cigarettes a day, ate junk food, never exercised, and lived to be ninety-five. This is who some people draw on when they don't want to drop the habits that aren't serving them. They loudly proclaim, "Well, my Uncle Willie did (fill in the bad habit here), and he lived to be ninety-five! So why should I change?" Simple.

You are not your Uncle Willie. And if you are betting your success and your life on it, I would *not* use Uncle Willie as your example. The most difficult yet most important thing to do is examine your habits and behaviors, understand where they come from, and decide which ones are helping you.

Let's say you want to break the habit of drinking four cans of soda every day. Rather than saying, "I'll never drink a can of soda again," setting yourself up for failure, drink one less can each day for two weeks (or longer if needed). Then you are down to three cans a day. Reduce your intake by another can each day for two more weeks or longer. Repeat until you are down to one or no cans each day.

All habits should be developed in ways that are sustainable. If the need for beverages is a strong habit, substitute water, tea, or even seltzer for soda. Let the acronym KISSES be your guide—Keep It Simple, Sustainable, Easy, and Supported.

Professor B.J. Fogg of Stanford University says creating "a real lifelong habit" requires training your brain to succeed by making small adjustments, then gaining "confidence from those successes." The Fogg Behavior Model focuses on three key elements:

1. *Motivation*—you are sufficiently motivated to change your behavior.
2. *Ability*—you must have the ability to do the new behavior.
3. *Trigger*—you need to find a trigger or prompt to do the behavior.

Here is an example. When I leave the coffee shop in the morning, I go home, set my clothes out for work, and then I work out. The trigger is coming home from the coffee shop, something I do almost every day. Even on the rare day when

I work from home, once I finish my coffee, I follow the same routine.

Find things you do every day that you can tie new positive behaviors to and create new positive habits. Remember to start small and build. I have a two-minute rule. It may sound silly, but it is effective. I will start by doing just two minutes of something. I do this because I don't have enough excuses to *not* do something for two minutes. You may also find that two minutes can turn into three, five, ten, or more. Always start at just two minutes. Try it. You'll like it!

Remember, big leaps rarely work because they are too scary, and our brain says, "Who are you kidding?" Plant a tiny, sustainable habit in the same spot where the old one resides, and it will grow without much coaxing. Pick something simple and easy to do. Hold yourself accountable and build on it every day.

Keep moving with small, simple, sustainable steps, and take note of what you are doing. Keep track and make the invisible (those old unconscious habits) visible (conscious new habits). One of the best parts about making small, sustainable changes is that it makes it easier to get back on track if you run off course. How you spend your time is an investment in your well-being. The habits you make can save you time and money. Heck, they can save your life and help create the you that you want.

Our habits are our companions, which can make them challenging. Changing them can be difficult, even painful. Yet sometimes, we have to go through some pain to create positive change. It may feel uncomfortable for a while, like anything new. For example, if you tried to write with your left hand and you are right-handed, it would feel weird. The same goes if you tried tying your shoes a different way. It will never be perfect, but after a while, it will be more comfortable. It is simply an adjustment on your journey to your new normal. I have been working on improving my cursive writing skills for taking notes, as it is supposed to be faster than printing. It's slow going and feels uncomfortable, yet I see the improvement already after just a couple of weeks.

The best way to get through this painful period is to just start. Often, the anticipation of an uncomfortable change (or any change) is the worst part. Rip off the Band-Aid and just start. Developing new habits taking just two minutes a day can pay off. Remember what I said earlier: Rome wasn't built in a day, but some part of it was. So get going. Do your part and always remember to be kind and patient with yourself!

Don't expect quick results. This is a journey. Many of us give up because there is no immediate payoff. Both our successes and failures are a series of small events that compound over time. It is making that cold call every day, saving a few quarters or dollars, adding that extra two minutes to your walk or workout, putting in the extra effort. Success is rarely immediate, and the good news is, that neither is failure. Every action we take or don't take will have an effect eventually. Often, we don't acknowledge the consequences of our actions—smoking, excessive drinking, excessive eating, not exercising, and goofing off at work—until it's too late. But it all catches up to us—the good, the bad, and the ugly. The fact that we don't see the quick results from our actions makes them easier to ignore. However, they still accumulate and compound over time whether you pay attention or choose to ignore them. Whether it's money or the steps you take to build a healthy relationship, there is always a cause and effect. And the effect of compounding is working in our lives every day, subtly. We cannot let the little things go unnoticed until it is too late.

Counting

Speaking of counting, you know on some level that you need to keep score. You need some form of measurement to track progress. If you don't do some type of measurement, how do you know if you have improved? Guess? If we only guess, odds are, we won't be right. Plus, when we guess, we usually guess in our favor, which can be worse. The only true way to know is if you count. When I say count, I mean activities or actions, like counting calories, sales calls, steps, minutes exercised, etc.

It is much harder to lie to yourself if you count. Look at the word ac*count*ability, and you will see the word count.

Make the invisible visible, meaning, make your goals visible, put them on paper, and display them; review them daily. You know the saying, "Out of sight out of mind." This will improve your life and take the guesswork out of where you are in terms of reaching your goal(s). Once again, when you make things visible and measurable, it is harder to lie to yourself. This applies to everything from counting calories to hugs. Counting is so important because everything compounds.

Many of us, myself included, tend to underestimate the amount we goof off, what we eat, how hard we work or study, and exaggerate our effort. Sometimes, it is easier not to know, so we avoid counting. Not knowing can make us feel more comfortable in the moment, but not knowing can cost us *big*! When we start counting, we also become more accountable. Numbers don't lie. Even something small, like making a schedule and keeping it out where you can see it. Paying attention to what you are spending your time doing. I never intend to be super-duper rigid, but this is something that can improve your chances of being happier, healthier, and more successful. That's the goal. You have to know in order to grow, so count everything because everything counts.

Counting is a process and may feel uncomfortable at first. Start slow, go slow, and grow. You will find when things are running better, you feel less stress. Remember, too, that a schedule is not a prison. It is a path—a path to a better life. And the funny thing is, it can give you more peace of mind and freedom.

The compound effect is always working. Whether you understand it, acknowledge it, ignore it, deny it, or minimize it, *it is working*. You cannot escape the effects of its power. Just because something hasn't happened yet doesn't mean it won't. Ignore the compound effect at your own peril.

Not so good

- Smoking
- Drinking to excess
- Not exercising
- Eating poorly
- Not saving and investing
- Ignoring a relationship
- Not doing your job
- Not improving yourself (you become obsolete)
- No plan
- No Schedule

Better

- Not smoking
- Casual drinking
- Light to moderate exercise
- Eating better
- Savings, investing, getting good advice
- Paying attention to your relationships
- Doing better at work

- Improving yourself (Personal development should end only on the day you die)
- Planning, scheduling
- Counting everything because everything counts

Action Step - Making the Invisible Visible

The simplest way to start the process is to make a simple chart using a notebook, an index card, or maybe even look for an app. Keep things where you can see them. You know the saying: "Out of sight, out of mind," so keep it visible. And remember, everything *compounds,* so count everything.

And don't take things too seriously. None of us is getting out of life alive.

Cause and Effect

Ralph Waldo Emerson said that cause and effect is the law of laws. The law is an absolute and undeviating truth in the world of thought as it is in the world of visible and material things. For every "Cause," there is an "Effect," and for every effect, there is a cause. If we look at anything that happens in our lives, whether the circumstances are desirable or undesirable, we are the ultimate root cause. With the exception of birth, genetics, and accidents, things don't just happen *to* you; they happen *because* of you. This is not about blaming or beating yourself up. This is about getting better by making small, smart improvements.

If you take a long, objective look at your life, you will find that you are where you are right now because of your choices and actions. I don't say this in a mean-spirited, blaming way. It's just something you have to realize. You are the cumulative effect of *all* causes, all of your choices, whether good, mediocre or maybe not so good. Research shows that we make 35,000 decisions per day. Most are unconscious, aka habits (the order in which you put on your clothes, for example). These constant choices create your life.

Head in Sand

As a whole, I think the world is in denial or maybe just intentionally ignoring the law of cause and effect. It is much easier to stick your head in the sand and make excuses than to acknowledge that we are, for the most part, the effect of our own causes. What we need to do is to look at our lives and say, "Yes, okay, I did that and ultimately ended up creating this. That's my part. Now I want to change, and I can make that change because I am responsible for my own life." Those constant choices *create* your life. In order to succeed at anything you must take a hundred percent responsibility for your life. I know, I know, I wrote it, and when I read it, it scared the *beep* out of me too!

Compound Effect

I tell myself, "If I write, I will improve my writing ability. If I exercise, I will improve my body, health, and attitude. If I learn and use what I learn, I will improve. I will increase my chances of success, improve both my personal and economic value, and I will have more joy and fulfillment in my life, and so will those around me." What is your mantra?

"You are the master of your thoughts, the molder of your character, and the maker and shaper of your condition, environment, and destiny."
~ James Allen

Nothing happens by accident. Your life didn't just happen. You created it. If you truly look deep enough, you will always find the common thread, the root cause of all your circumstances. Understand that there can be no effect without a cause. Thus, if we want a certain effect, we should place our focus and our energy on finding the cause. And if we can duplicate the cause, then we can duplicate the effect. When you do that, you'll discover what and why you hold yourself back, and then you will set yourself free. Remember this, *the truth will set you free, but first, it will piss you off.* Don't get stuck in the latter.

Tools and Reminders

- Pay attention.
- Schedule your time (structure creates success and freedom).
- Make the invisible visible.
- Count and be accountable.
- Make a promise or behavior contract with yourself.
- Have frequent checkpoints.

- Count everything because everything counts.
- Start small; make it easy to do.
- Make it sustainable; remember KISSES— Keep It Simple, Sustainable, Easy, and Supported

"It's not the big things that add up in the end; it's the hundreds, thousands, or millions of little things that separate the ordinary from the extraordinary."

~ Darren Hardy, *The Compound Effect: Jumpstart Your Income, Your Life, Your Success*

7

Law of Association

Never underestimate the power of association.
All of your associations have an impact on you.

"Keep away from people who try to belittle your ambitions. Small people always do that, but the really great make you feel that you too can become great. When you are seeking to bring big plans to fruition, it is important with whom you regularly associate."

~ Mark Twain

In the mid-1980s and 1990s, racquetball was big. I started playing and eventually was playing four-to-six times per week. It was a lot of fun. I became a solid "B" player (before I discovered the power of coaching). However, I noticed that when I played an "A" player, my game got better. When playing with the "big guns," I had to be better just to stay on the scoreboard.

Occasionally, I played with my mentor, Les, who was twenty-five years older but still an avid and excellent player. He plaelonyed every day at lunchtime. I'll call him a finesse player, whereas I was more a power player (or, more accurately, a bull-in-a-china-shop player). Les would run me all around the court. He ran me up and down, back and forth, and sideways. He ran me ragged and kicked my butt every single time we played, and I don't think he even broke a sweat.

But every time I played him, I learned something, and I got a little better. I never beat him. Maybe if I stuck with it long enough, I could have, or he would have gotten too old to beat me. Even though I improved overall, I noticed that when I played with "C" players, my game was worse, sometimes even horrible. I became lackadaisical and stopped paying close attention to the game because I knew I could beat them. As a result, these lesser players would sometimes beat me because I wasn't bringing my "A" game or even my "B" game.

Who we associate with in every game we play, including the game of life, affects how we play the game and eventually who we become. Ask yourself this: are the other players on your court improving your game or bringing you down? If you want to be an "A" player, you need to play with "A" players. Here's a good saying to remember. If you run with the chickens, you'll be scratching in the dirt. If you hang with eagles, you'll be soaring in the sky.

This is the Law of Association—a little-known and much-unheeded law about life, success, happiness, and health. It is the cosmic version of that sage parental advice: pick your friends wisely. It is based on the fact that who we spend our time with plays a large part in how we shape our world. The people you associate with become a part of your external environment, which affects your internal one and, inevitably, your prosperity—and that includes your health, wealth, happiness, and the value you bring to the world.

Take a moment to think this over. If you hung out with Bill Gates, Warren Buffett, or Elon Musk, do you think your financial life might be different? What about your thinking, ideas, and views? Stop here and think about why your associations, tribes, or gangs are so important. It is because there are a lot of deep evolutionary reasons like survival. Our associations mean *everyone* in our lives and environment because they all influence *us*. It is part of our unconscious need and drive to fit in with the people around us. We need to be accepted. We need to be liked. And so, below the level of awareness, we conform in many ways. We become like our tribe.

But we also have the gift of free will. And that allows possibility, within limits, and sometimes even apart from any limits, for us to choose our tribe. I say within limits because we have to work our way into some tribes. And Elon is not taking my calls. Oh well.

"Isolation is the enemy of excellence."
~ Aaron Walker

It's crucial to know who is in your GANG. That acronym, Goal Achieving Nudging Group, represents people you hang with who have compatible tastes, goals, and mutual interests. It's crucial because the people you associate with determine the person you will become. If you are in sales, hang out with the top salespeople, not the water-cooler whiners. Look for friends who have goals and are primed for success.

The people around you should be individuals you can learn from, who inspire you to reach your goals, and who you also inspire and help. You won't find millionaires hanging around with bums unless it's the holidays and they happen to be related to them. As Groucho Marx said, "I don't want to belong to any club that would accept me as a member."

When we associate with people of real wisdom and virtue, people who are accomplished and knowledgeable, we become encouraged to pursue our quest for greatness. The path to success becomes easier. Why, then, should we ever settle for less?

I have always liked the quote by Peter J. Daniels, Australian businessman, speaker, and author of *Miss Phillips You Were Wrong*. He wrote, "I associate with people who have empires in their minds." What do the people you associate with have in their minds?

We need support around us. This is often undervalued. We all need a brotherhood or sisterhood, a GANG. That is why Navy Seals, Marines, and special forces dominate. They have lots of support. They are a team and a great GANG.

Have you developed resources to help support you and keep you accountable—to nudge you? Isn't it time to find your GANG? Having the right support will keep you going. Having the right people to help you generate that energy can be lifesaving. Very few, if any, of us have the power to continue totally by ourselves. We need others.

With the help of your GANG, you will determine your momentum. That momentum can be slow or fast. It is up to you. The secret is sustainability—the ability to keep going. The pace depends on you, your GANG, and your goals. If the general momentum is moving forward quickly, the GANG will pick up the pace and move faster. But a slower-moving GANG can slow down everyone around them. It's like when you're in traffic and, for no good reason, someone is driving 40 in a 55-mph zone—just going slow, clogging up all the lanes. You have unintentionally joined the wrong traffic GANG. However, it only takes one person to push or nudge the group to pick up speed. If everyone simply sped up a little or drove in the proper lane, the traffic would flow smoothly again, and you would reach your destination (goal).

Once you have examined your GANG(s), take a look at their momentum. Ask yourself, "Is this the pace I want to be going? Am I in the right lane?"

> "You will be the same person in five years that you are today, except for the people you associate with and the books you read."
> ~ Charles "Tremendous" Jones

Environment (Culture)

I grew up with a guy who was good-looking, strong, hardworking, and smart. However, he always seemed to be in trouble, and everyone expected poor behavior from him. He became an alcoholic and did lots of stupid—very stupid—things for many years. Soon, the community expected that he would always be a bum.

At one point, there was an incident with local officials, and he was asked to leave town. He moved sixty miles away. Then something magical happened. He changed. Being in a new environment where no one knew him or had expectations, his view of himself changed. He got sober, joined the volunteer fire department, started a small business, and became a respected member of the community.

I ran into him a few weeks ago, and he was still doing well, still sober. When back in his old stomping grounds, he seemed uncomfortable because he had left that bum behind. In a new setting with new expectations, he changed his life for the better. Sometimes that is what it takes—a new environment where we can start over with a clean slate.

Our environment has a great deal to do with our success in attaining our goals. For example, if the gym is an hour out of your way or cluttered with uncommitted people, it becomes a social club. It will be much more difficult to sustain our workout routine. Please don't get me wrong. Our connections are great. We need them. Yet, we need to get done what we need to get done.

In the last month or so, I have changed coffee shops. I still go to my former place a couple of times per week, not totally breaking my connections. I changed because they installed a television, which is not good for my focus and getting things done. Remember, "Be selfish with your time and kind to people." Working from home serves many people well because there are fewer distractions. I struggle with that because I feel guilty about not being at the office. But I do get more done in coffee shops and at home. The goal is productivity—using your time the best way you can.

You can start by being a "Blockhead." Your environment is crucial to your productivity. Few people have the massive willpower and discipline to constantly perform at high levels. If more people did, the world would be filled with healthy, motivated, and successful people. And don't feel bad about being selfish with your time; it's yours. You are achieving your goals. And for those around you, you are a beacon of light on how to live a better life.

Whether we are at work, home, school, or out on the playing field, we act a little differently or display certain personality traits more exuberantly in one setting versus another due to our surroundings and our desire to fit in. For example, we may show our competitive streak and more confidence on the playing field than at home with our family. It occurs not only because of the environment but because of our need to fit in and blend with our surroundings. The energy of our group, team, or GANG is very important. We must create our environment, or our environment will create us.

It is crucial to pay attention to your environment. If you keep your environment small, you are promoting small thinking. Your exposure to new ideas and concepts will be small. You may not be exposed to new ways of thinking. What you want are bigger thoughts.

By structuring your surroundings, you can eliminate distractions and become more effective in reaching your goals. For example, a key tip for losing weight is to be picky in the food you keep on hand. If you don't have junk food, you won't be tempted to eat it. You reduce a potential distraction. In addition, you don't have to rely on willpower all the time. Willpower comes in a limited supply.

If you are trying to run more, you could keep your running socks and shoes right by the door, so you can't avoid them. When you are ready to get going, you won't be wasting time searching for what you need, which sometimes affords you the time to demotivate—to find excuses not to run.

Set yourself up for success. Your structure can determine behavior. How you structure your environment can make you more successful. Remember, it's in your control. For example, I was the oldest of five boys. My father was a mean and brutal alcoholic. I had an awkward overbite, and I struggled with reading. School proved to be one of the great difficulties in my childhood. It's no surprise that I didn't get very far while living in that home environment.

However, when I was in the military, I thought and acted much differently simply because of the environment—the people around me. We adopted military attitudes, not only in what we did but in how we did it. Because of my military experience, I learned how to have more control over my environment and how to shape myself into someone who could reach goals and succeed.

I surround myself with inspiring quotes because they provide constant reminders and positive affirmations. I hang them on the walls or stick them on the dashboard of my car and computer monitor. I even have erasable markers in the shower so I can write notes on the wall. I don't want an idea to get away. I constantly take motivational showers—reading, doing things that challenge my fears, and disputing negative thoughts that arise. I stay near motivated people and ask them for support when necessary. If I do that every day, I improve every day. And you know what? No matter what happens, I feel better because I am living internally, not externally. It isn't up to the world to make me happy; it is up to me to be happy.

I use a calendar and block off time for exercise, writing, work, and free time. And when it is free time, I am just that—free to do whatever I please because I have blocked off all the other things I need to achieve in my day. Those tasks won't be weighing on my mind during my free time. All these things, schedules, post-it notes, and emailing myself are examples of small things I do to keep myself on track and set myself up for success.

Creating structure will give you freedom and success. Having a new structure to live within can be very uncomfortable in the beginning. But once you get used to it, you can make your environment work for you instead of the other way around.

Remember this as you continue on your journey forward. What you accomplish in the next two years will be determined by three things:

1. The books you read, things you listen to, and what you watch
2. The people you associate with and the environment you shape
3. The actions you take

Always remember that you can choose your environment and associations. If you associate with small thinking people, you will think small. And when you do change, it will feel weird, scary, and uncomfortable. However, that will change over time.

Tools and Reminders

- Be selfish with your time and kind to people.
- Associate with people who care enough about you to tell you the truth.
- Have a backup plan. "No battle plan survives contact with the enemy," Helmuth von Moltke, *German general at the start of the First World War,* said. We all get off track, so have a plan, someone you can call or change your environment. This is where accountability partners and goal buddies help.
- Create a Promise Contract with yourself about what you want to achieve and when it will be done.
- Find a coach. The cost versus what you get and can become is invaluable. And once you develop a new habit, skill, or path, it is yours forever.
- Structure keeps you sane. Be a Blockhead. Block out the times you are most productive and make a list of priority things to be done. Do less important things when your energy is low. Much of this goes back to paying attention and knowing yourself.
- Control your environment as much as possible (people, places, things).
- Have a "get back on track" plan. Success takes time—a long-term commitment to doing the work. It takes discipline and courage.
- *Remember*, misery loves company. And so does success.

It is a funny thing about people; they will let themselves down before they let the team down. We all do better when someone is watching, when we have a team, a GANG.

We all need a push!

The Eagles

Come to the edge, he said.
They said, we are afraid.
Come to the edge, he said.
They came
He pushed them, and they flew.
~ Guillaume Apollinaire

Chapter

8

Design Your Life Your Way

"The greater danger for most of us lies not in
setting our aim too high and falling short, but
in setting our aim too low and achieving our
mark."
~ Michelangelo

"If you always do what you've always done, you will always
get what you always got."
~ Henry Ford

Maybe you had goals of your own at one time; maybe you
had a dream; maybe you've just given up on your dreams, so
you plod along living someone else's dream. And make no
mistake about it, if you aren't following your designed life,
you are following someone else's.

It is important for you to continually think about and take steps toward fashioning the life you want to live. That is why it is vital to make the invisible visible, making the invisible visible means knowing what you want, knowing your goals and objectives, and getting *very clear* about your end product. Also, visible means posting your goals in places where you can see and review them frequently. At a bare minimum, review them monthly. Even better, do it weekly and review some daily. And it is vital to ensure that your goals are manageable. KISSES—Keep It Simple, Sustainable, Easy, and Supported.

Beware of too many goals. I often need a reminder because this is usually my problem. Like many people who have a lot of goals because they want to do everything, sometimes, nothing much happens. It is a form of self-defeating or self-sabotaging behavior. Yes, I know one or two goals aren't as exciting as ten or fifteen, or even fifty. However, accomplishing two instead of none could be cool! It's like an old saying that I *hate*. "A hunter who chases two rabbits catches none."

With all the information, options, and opportunities available to us twenty-four seven, why do so few people take advantage of this when trying to attain a goal? You can learn and do almost anything. Yes, anything. So why don't you? If you can answer that question honestly without blame, shame, guilt, or excuses, you will be at the beginning of a new life— the life you want.

My answer to the question above is simple, familiar, and of course, right. It is fear! You are:

- Afraid to try
- Afraid to fail
- Afraid to succeed
- Afraid of what other people will think

Design Your Life Your Way

According to Shad Helmstetter in his book, *Who Are You Really and What Do You Want?* it is a fact of human psychology that people whose lives are not self-directed live lives directed by the world around them or by someone else. If you don't take charge, you will be like a tumbleweed in the desert, rolling in whichever direction the wind is blowing. No matter how far-fetched it seems, you'll be amazed at what happens when you set a goal and take steps toward it. As Emerson said, "Once you decide, the universe conspires to make it happen." Just be careful not to ignore it, push it away, give up, or run away.

A common phrase a while back was Big Hairy Audacious Goals or BHAGs. And while I think it's great to have big dreams and goals, such an approach rarely works. People are overwhelmed before they start. Not good! Perhaps the more obvious and better solution is:

1. Use KISSES
2. Decide on something
3. Start small
4. Keep going
5. Find a way to get the support you need (*ask*)
6. Find your GANG

When people start to take on too much, it often becomes a disaster. They get discouraged and either quit or give up, and nothing happens. Then they beat themselves up and classify themselves as losers. It's more destructive than it is helpful. That is why it's important to start small and make it sustainable. Always remember the last "S" in KISSES, SUPPORTED. And if you mess up, *get up*. You are, after all, human. Remember how hard it was to learn to read? What if you gave up? You wouldn't have been able to read this.

Take water, for instance. Water is one of the most powerful forces in the universe. It can change the course of rivers or destroy communities. It can also feed us, nurture us, and give us great joy. Water usually moves slowly. It can take millions of years to carve out a canyon. Yet each day, water moves a few grains of sand or sediment, smoothing a rock and cutting new paths. If there's an obstacle in the way, water goes over it, under it, or around it and keeps going. Even if the obstacle slows the water down, eventually, it weaves its way past it, creating change slowly but surely, slow sustainable, steady movement.

Like water, you may have a goal to carve out. Suppose you want to write a book. The typical book could be 30,000 to 60,000 words or about 100 to 200 pages. If you wrote just one page a week, in three years, you'd get the job done— slow, steady, sustainable.

Once you know what you want, make a plan. Know that most likely, the plan may not work out the first time or may need adjustments. It will evolve but eventually move you forward. Remember Newton's law, "A body in motion stays in motion."

HOW DO YOU EAT AN ELEPHANT

There is a motivational saying; "How do you eat an elephant? One bite at a time." Trite, but true. Trying to eat an elephant too fast, taking too huge of a bite, or many bites at one time, you could choke. That's what happens to our goals and dreams when we try to bite off more than we can chew. Trust me. I'm an expert in this. I try to do a hundred things at one time. Somehow, I've managed to survive, but I know I could do better by focusing more, taking smaller bites, or slowing down.

When it comes to setting your goals, eat your elephant one bite at a time. Make a plan today. Write this, for example, "This is what I will do (be specific) today. And this is what I do (be specific) tomorrow." What gets scheduled gets done. That way, you won't choke on your list. Again, your schedule is a path, not a prison. Sometimes adjustments are necessary, especially when the unexpected happens. Allow time for glitches. Having too much going on can cause your brain to overload. Your system shuts down, self-doubt, SDBs, or even panic may set in, and you can't do anything. So always remember to take small bites (steps) consistently. It's about sustainability. KISSES.

You define what success is for you. It may differ from how I define it. Success is whatever it means to you. You need to learn to look at success without fear. Take your blinders off and recognize what you need to do to get out of your own way.

There is no straight line or one-size-fits-all formula. Find what works best for you by examining your past experiences, style, and preferences. That will help you create your personal formula. The key is to find your way and keep doing it.

Examining what worked:

- o When have you been most productive?
- o When have you accomplished the most?

- o What was the environment?
- o Who was involved?
- o How did you hold yourself accountable?

Take Action NOW

What are your goals, dreams, your vision? If there were no boundaries and you could do whatever you want to do in life, what would you do?

Get some paper and start by writing down what you want. Avoid censoring your thoughts. Try not to allow your doubts to stop you from writing a thought that enters your mind. Remember, this is for you. No one else needs to see it, and it may change as time passes, so don't be shy about it. Read and refer back to your list weekly to keep your goals, dreams, and vision at the forefront of your mind. It only takes five minutes. Make the invisible visible. Remember to take action, maintain, and nurture a strong belief in yourself. You *will* make it happen!

Why is reading your dream, vision, or goal list important? Like the old saying, "Out of sight, out of mind." If we don't pay attention and stay focused, we can never accomplish what we want.

Let me give you an example. When I was forty-one, and again at fifty-one, I did life vision and goals exercises. Questions like, pretend it is ten years from now.

- What are your favorite things?
- What have you accomplished?
- What are you sorry you didn't do or wish you had done?

It was the last question that got me.

One day while cleaning my desk, in the bottom of a drawer, I found two goalsetting exercises I had done ten-plus years earlier. I hadn't looked at either document for many years. Surprisingly, the answers were very similar. One question was, "Sorry I didn't, wish I had," and it asked you to project ten years into the future and make a list of things you didn't do but wished you had. Like most people, I did the exercises, put the list in a drawer, and forgot about it. As I reviewed the list, I noticed a few things; the lists were almost identical, and there were also some interesting insights. I had projected I would be earning $125,000. I actually earned $124,500 that year. I wish I had projected a bigger number. Below are three other goals that had not yet been completed . . . or even started.

1. Take the kids to California.
2. Write a book.
3. Do seminars and workshops on personal development.

I took the kids to California that summer and started writing, joined Toastmasters, and developed a workshop. I planned and advertised the workshop even though I had no workshop. Two people signed up, and each paid $99 for the six-week, one-hour-per-week program. I had to hustle and create material for the workshop, which I have improved over the years. The interesting thing is that both attendees made positive changes. One sought out his estranged biological father; the other started a photography business.

Now I am on my third book, and people love my workshops. Also, I have been running a mastermind* group for workshop attendees for over ten years and recently started doing stand-up comedy.

Stand-up comedy wasn't on the list but was always there somewhere hidden, suppressed, denied, in the recesses of my mind. The reason it was hidden, like so many other things I hide, is because I thought I couldn't do stand-up. Basically, it boiled down to this. I was chicken, so I made up excuses. I mean, I had reasons.

When I planned to open my own insurance agency, I wanted the office on my mother's sun porch. (She didn't know that was my plan.) Come to think of it, there wasn't even an outside door to that room. Imagine my customers walking through my parents' living room to get to the sun porch! Ahh . . . my office! That was my dream, my goal, my plan for success.

That was not my father's idea of success. He thought I should follow his path: go to work at Monsanto and work lots of overtime. My thinking was if I were going to work overtime, it would be for me.

I suppose you could say my ideas and goals were fuzzy. I needed to learn to un-fuzz them because fuzzy goals create fuzzy results. Yet, I trudged onward, and the universe began to respond with opportunities.

As my insurance business grew, I decided to give real estate another go, so I started my own company. As the business grew, I added a manager, and eventually, we had twenty agents.

At the same time, I decided to build on speculation (building without a buyer) with my friend Dave. Things went well until the summer of 1988, when the housing market collapsed overnight. Dave and I got stuck with two houses we couldn't sell. Those houses cost us $120,000 out of pocket to carry until they sold, three years later. In today's dollars, that would be $200,000. The good news is we did sell them, and while builders lost their properties to foreclosure and bankruptcy, we survived, even though it did

---

*A mastermind group is a peer-to-peer mentoring group used to help members grow and develop with input, advice, accountability, and support from the other group members. The concept was coined in 1925 by author Napoleon Hill in his book *The Law of Success* and described in more detail in his 1937 book Think and Grow Rich.

cost us all the money we earned on the prior houses we built. What's the lesson? I believe to this day, if I had had a mentor, a trusted advisor, or different people around me, I would have dumped those houses at a smaller loss immediately, taken the hit, and been better off. Who you associate with is crucial and can be costly.

You create and design your destiny. You can whine all you want, but you choose the life you want, and you create it. Everything, at some level, is a choice. Your choice. People often don't realize that when they are designing their life— their destiny. Everything you do, think, and say, as well as everything you don't do, think, and say, determines your destiny.

Too often, we are stuck in the idea that we think someone else or something else is creating our future, so we fail to take charge and consciously design it ourselves. So, why not take a chance on yourself and your future? Create a blueprint for your life and design it your way. The worst thing that could happen is you start over. But even then, the experience will have made you smarter and stronger.

Your Personal Blueprint

No one would build a house or a large building without a vision of its design, size, and location. Before building a commercial building, for example, the visionary would have an architect draw blueprints providing detailed plans for the foundation, room sizes, plumbing, wiring, and exterior design—maybe even build a scale model.

You are the visionary of your life. You are the architect of your personal blueprint. Designing your life your way requires conscious and sometimes courageous thinking. With focused commitment, you can build the life you want.

What does a great life look like to you? In the key areas of your life, between one and ten, ten being the highest, what score do you give your current life?

Eric Hoffer said, "We lie loudest when we lie to ourselves." That's why I recommend rating yourself with a quantitative measure. For example, maybe you rate your relationship a Level 5, and you want to find a way to increase that number to a Level 7, 8, 9, or even a 10. Recognizing that area needs improvement will help spark your drive to take action.

What does a great relationship look like to you? What changes do you need to make, or steps can you take to improve what you have now? Writing all of this on paper will help you clarify your goal and the steps you need to take.

Building Blocks of Prosperity

Prosperity/Success

More Persistence & Patience, Discipline

More Action

More Accountability & Support

Checkpoints/ Adjustments

Persistence, Patience, Discipline, Accountability & Support

Action/Implement Plan

Plan

Decide

Want/Desire Dream/Vision

For every level, there is another devil.

You Define Success

Your goal is to define success for yourself, not to depend on what someone else tells you it should mean. You choose your life's design, and you also determine the outcome or the final product (no guarantees). No one is going to hand you success or the life you want. You must create it yourself. You must earn it. No one is coming to rescue you.

Embarking on your journey to success takes work, time, persistence, practice, failures, learning, more work, and, yes, sacrifice. If you want something, you must be willing to pay the price. Regardless of the wins, you celebrate and the challenges you encounter, the true prize will always be the self-knowledge and understanding that you gain along the way. Yes, each step, failure, lesson, or success adds to you and makes a better "You." And yes, sometimes it will suck, so you always need to take a deep breath and keep picking yourself up. So Suck It Up, Cupcake!

When you begin your travels, you must prepare for those outside voices that will try to convince you to turn around. Even people who care about you may be conflicted, confused, and concerned because of their own limiting beliefs and fear. As Emerson wrote, "Envy is ignorance; imitation is suicide." Envy is a lack of appreciation of your special gifts; imitating another person destroys your originality. You have something unique, original, and great to express. Again, in the words of Emerson, genius is simply to "believe your own thought, to believe that what is true for you in your private heart is true for all." Notice he said your *private* heart, the one to which we rarely listen.

Discipline

"The purpose of discipline is to live more fully, not less."
~ Master Po, *in the pilot of the TV series Kung Fu*

What would your life be like if you had self-discipline in every aspect of it—your health, finances, career, relationships? The world belongs to the disciplined. The paradox of self-discipline is that it creates freedom. We, however, tend to think it's the opposite. We think it creates drudgery, so that's what we have in our minds. We need to realize that discipline makes life easier and will likely keep us from getting exhausted or burned out.

It has been said that discipline is the glue that holds everything together, making everything else work. And yes, I know I am repeating myself, but it is important to get this. I think most people hide from discipline mostly because of what they believe. I also fall into this trap, often equating discipline with drudgery, blood, sweat, tears, rigidity, or an unforgiving and unending grind. I tend to fear boredom, and discipline to me smacks of boredom. Yet, when I am disciplined, and everything gets done, I feel so much better. Some personality styles take on discipline easier than others. But if you don't have some level of self-discipline, other principles of success will not work. The good news is discipline can be increased over time. That is when you may need to reach out for help from an accountability partner, buddy, friend, coach, mentor, boss, or coworker. Remember, support is important, and a good philosophy is to have people who care about you enough to give you a kick in the "you know what" when you need one.

Planning

You wouldn't go shopping without a plan and a list, yet most people live life without them. Planning helps us make better choices. Planning helps us avoid the distractions that push us off course. People spend more time planning a two- week vacation than they do planning their future, their finances, or their life's design.

People who have defined goals are more likely to have more control over their time, business, career, and lives. When asked what had the greatest impact on their productivity, many successful people say they invested time planning activities every day. The existence of a quality business plan or life plan has the greatest impact on an individual's ability to successfully prioritize and grow. In developing any plan, it's important to identify objectives, steps, and checkpoints. The same is true when developing a plan for your life.

All plans need to be adjusted from time to time. Life has a way of throwing curveballs. This is where flexibility and adaptability come into play. It does not mean you should not plan; it means you need to be open to change. New opportunities or challenges may arise that you never thought of before. Having the attitude that you can handle whatever happens means you can adjust when necessary.

What are you trying to accomplish, and why? List the top three objectives for your business, your career, and your life for the next three years. Answer these questions first:

- Why am I setting these objectives?
- Do the objectives fit with my life plans, values, goals, and vision?
- Are the objectives in line with each other and my goals?

Here is an example of how an objective might appear:

- o **Objective:** hire two additional team members.
- o **Why:** To enable me to increase the number of clients served, to allow for greater flexibility with my time,

to begin grooming my successor, and to have more time and fun.

So, think about your plan. Keep your goals in front of you. Build discipline and accountability in your life.

Goals or Wishes

A goal is something we take action on. A wish is something we just whimsically think about. "Oh, I wish I had a million dollars." "I wish I had a better body." "I wish I had a better relationship." Wishes are goals without plans, objectives, or actions. Wishes have no wings.

You have to continually take steps toward fashioning the life you want to live. Things are always changing; you are always changing, and sometimes our dreams and goals may change. If it is a conscious choice, an acceptable choice, that's okay. But if you allow other people to make choices for you or allow emotions such as fear to make choices for you, you've stopped living your life your way. That is when you need to take a step back and examine your direction.

The earlier you start on your designed path, the better it is. You will have more time to work at achieving your goals because, as I said, things do change. If they do, you may have to modify your plans temporarily or *find new ways* to work toward your goals. It's the people who keep moving forward who ultimately succeed. I believe such people live the happiest and most fulfilling lives. They are continually working, adapting, and struggling toward their desired lives. Always remember the value of the process and the struggles because they *make us stronger*. We often look back on those times with pride and laughter.

Life is meant to be lived to the fullest until the very end. Those who do so have few regrets and seem happier and more at peace with life and themselves. Even though life may sometimes give you a flat tire, send you on a detour, or give you transmission trouble, you can always find a way. Keep a spare in your trunk, find alternate routes, and have your tranny checked.

Schedule that Goalanoscopy. Attend a workshop or online seminar. Ask for help. It doesn't matter how or what you want. Just take action! Find A Way!

It comes down to a few basic questions you need to ask yourself. "What do I really want?" "What am I willing to do?" "How much desire do I have to get what I want?" You have to be crystal clear about the answers to those questions, for they are the foundation in your blueprint for the life you are designing for yourself.

And remember to be grateful. We live in a time when there are more options and opportunities for all of us—if we look for them.

Take Action Now

Stop wishing. A wish is not a plan. A wish is not action. A wish is a fantasy and delusion, so stop it.

- Stop wishing you were smarter. You are smart enough.
- Stop wishing you had more time. Plan to use your time better.
- Stop wishing you had that job, career, or business, and make it happen.
- Stop wishing and start saying, "I am doing."
- Stop listening to and associating with going-nowhere people.
- Stop lying and deluding yourself.
- Stop wishing things were different. Start making yourself better.
- Stop wasting time.

- Stop whining and complaining.
- Stop making excuses.
- Stop playing the blame game.
- Stop missing exercise time.

START giving yourself credit. START understanding that the only way to be above average is to stop being average. START now!

Deliberate Practice

The world is filled with gifted people with enormous potential. We all have some talents. Yes, you and I are talented. The key is to find your talent and then get out of your own way, develop it, and use it. Don't get me wrong. You still need to work on things. The effort is key. One of the things I have observed and find encouraging—no, find exciting—is, for the most part, talent will only get you so far. The balance is work, discipline, and deliberate practice. I can do that; we all can do that!

Deliberate practice is a specific practice or set of practices that improve very small elements of whatever you're doing a little at a time and perfecting them. It requires coaching, attention, and intention. And because it requires extreme focus, it can only be done in short spurts.

Here are several examples from K. Anders Ericsson, author of *Peak: Secrets from The New Science of Expertise.* Ericsson espouses deliberate practice, which entails:

- well-defined, **specific** goals
- full engagement and high concentration
- feedback
- getting out of one's comfort zone
- chunking: breaking down the overall skill into sub-skills and training them separately—as opposed to practicing the full skill repeatedly
- identifying and eliminating mistakes.

Yes, some people have innate strengths, skills, and talents. According to Professor Ericsson, those are more helpful at the beginning of any activity. Yet, at some point, there is a crossover where discipline and deliberate practice take a person to the next level. So, there is no substitute for hard work, discipline, and deliberate practice.

The rarity of a so-called genius or savant is huge, and if you read Ericsson's work, he shows how even a savant uses deliberate practice. I find that incredibly encouraging because it means there are far more possibilities open to most of us. I think the problem lies in the fact that what we see in life and in the media is the finished product, not the beginning. You don't see Michael Jordan missing baskets or Amy Schumer or Jerry Seinfeld flubbing onstage. You missed those early years when they did. Now when you see them, you conjure the image of the polished finished product and proclaim, "I could never do that." I will bet you there was a time when they thought the same thing. I am willing to bet they could tell you a ton of stories about their fears, doubts, struggles, mistakes, embarrassments, and failures. I have been doing some open mic standup comedy lately, and I often see professionals coming in to practice new material.

And yes, sometimes they stink. What they do, however, is learn and improve from it.

If you want to know the secret to getting better at anything, it is discipline and deliberate practice. As my drum instructor, Rob Sebetes, always says, "It isn't practice that makes better or perfect. It is *correct practice* that makes better," aka Deliberate Practice.

I think we often have talents and potential that go unused, unrecognized, or undervalued, mostly by ourselves. Most of us have a propensity for some things more than others. The goal is to find those gifts, talents, or potential and acknowledge, develop, and use them. Yes, everyone has some talent. Everyone has abilities or potential. But without a certain amount of discipline, without practice, those skills and talents never develop—and that is the saddest story of our world.

You get the point. Whatever your talent, maybe you can't do it well today, tomorrow, or even the next day. But if you are diligent and keep at it, improving a little with each try, one day you will excel. It doesn't matter what you want. Practice applies to everything—music, athletics, business, sales, medicine, art, organizing, managing, public speaking, standup comedy, programming, etc. You will be able to do it better.

What might your talents be? Here's a list to get you thinking about what you have that you may not be acknowledging.

Organization	Leading Problem-solving
Writing (or proofreading, editing)	Working well and quickly in emergencies
Communication Clarifying	Applying logic and order
Taking A & B and tweaking it and making it into C	Mathematical ability
	Languages
Following logical paths	Showing empathy Adapting
Seeing what needs to be done	Cleaning/neatness Cooking
Helping others stay on track	Seeing details Listening
Making or editing videos	Welcoming or connecting
Researching or investigating	Good at starting
Working with your hands	Good at finishing Coming up
Great hand/eye coordination	with ideas Implementing
Being creative in art, music, design	Coaching or mentoring
	Analyzing
Getting things done on time	Big-picture thinking
Building things	**And the list goes on and on**
Spatial skills	
Picturing or imagining things	
Decorating/mixing colors	
Patience	

I recommend everyone read *Peak: Secrets from The New Science of Expertise*. It dispels many myths surrounding ability and talent versus hard work and introduces what the author calls "deliberate practice." Deliberate practice creates a new thought habit of *I can*. In Ericsson's book, you will find all the details and information you need to help you along your way. The exciting truth is that most of us can learn or do almost anything at a very high level, but it requires time, energy, and deliberate practice.

Now, all that being said, if you are not planning to be world-class at anything, for example, an Olympic athlete, play at Carnegie Hall or write a best-selling novel, there is still a great deal to be gained from deliberate practice. There are many levels to which you can aspire. If you want to improve at anything, doing the right kind of practice, even for a short time, can significantly improve your outcome.

Receiving coaching in any area will be a shortcut to improvement. For example, my friend Charlie and I are experienced public speakers and can significantly impact a novice speaker's skill level in a few sessions. And for my part, I have had many hours of great coaching from my friends Margo Chevers and Ken Crannell, both world-class speakers, and coaches. What a difference it made!

Great coaching is always a shortcut to where you want to go. However, it does require you to get out of your comfort zone. It took me a month to work up the courage to call Ken about coaching.

When I finally spoke to him, he said, "Send me a video of a speech, and I will review it and let you know if I will work with you." Let me know. Holy crap! I had to audition for coaching. I sent him a DVD, and two weeks later, it was returned with three double-sided pages of notes followed by a call from Ken.

"You have a lot of things wrong with your speaking," he said. "The good news is it's all fixable."

During the sessions that followed, Ken often apologized for being so tough. "That's why I am here," I said.

I like what NFL Hall-of-Famer, Emmitt Smith, said about success. "All men and women are created equal; some just work harder in pre-season." You do have to work harder, which by the way, is part of working smarter. I mean, who wants to work dumber? Working harder is not as difficult as people might want you to believe. Working harder isn't a big deal unless you make it a bigger deal than it is. And, yes, it won't always be easy. That is why you need to be clear about what you want. Of course, if you are going to put in the effort, it should be toward something you really want to do. That is why paying attention and knowing yourself is so important.

Mentors and Coaches: Finding the Cracks We Don't See

If there is one lesson, I wish I had learned sooner in life, it would be the importance of having mentors and coaches. They can be extremely valuable. Unlike a family member or close friend, your coach is not emotionally involved with you. Your coach can see and point out areas in your life or skills you want to build that you may deny or not want to acknowledge. Denial and delusion usually spell one thing, D-I-S-A-S-T-E-R.

Here is an example. When I listed the two houses I built just before the housing market collapsed, I could have bailed out and taken a $10,000 loss per house. Instead, I held onto them, which resulted in a $125,000 loss. I was too close to the issue and in denial about the long-term risks. Some of my friends and family agreed with me, which isn't always helpful. A mentor, coach, or experienced business advisor standing on the outside, holding an objective point of view, might have helped me realize the extent of the consequences I was facing by holding the assets.

A great coach or mentor will make you see and do what they know you can do, especially when you don't. Even when you know something is good for you, the fear of showing imperfections, failure, quitting, or giving up is terrifying. Coaches and mentors (bosses and managers, too) can help us build accountability and give us support to move forward, especially when we enter the "Valley of Dead Dreams." Remember the last "S" in KISSES, Support.

Discipline

The world belongs to the disciplined. I know, this scares me too! The paradox of self-discipline is this; discipline creates freedom. It also creates good, better, and best outcomes. Discipline creates greatness. We, however, tend to think the opposite. We think it creates drudgery, so that's what we have in our minds. We need to realize discipline will make our lives easier or better and will likely keep us from getting exhausted and burned out. Discipline helps us to be happier and healthier. Working toward something we want, and making improvements, even when we get frustrated, is usually the most fulfilling time in our lives.

Discipline is the glue that holds everything together, making everything else work. Yet I think most people run from discipline, mostly because of what they believe. I often equate it with drudgery, an unending grind. At least for me, I tend to fear boredom, coupled with a little ADHD and SOS (Shiny Object Syndrome), and FOMO (Fear of Missing Out), so discipline scares me even though I like the results. I also think some personality styles take to discipline more easily than others. Of course, that is just my guess, or maybe my excuse.

Success in life is only rented, and the rent is due every day. Success in your relationships, business, finances, and health doesn't just happen. Every day, you must pay the rent again. If you don't have discipline, none of the principles of success will work. Discipline is important!

Remember these words from Professor Jordon Peterson; if you want to do anything, "start by doing it badly," and "if you stand still, you are moving backward."

With deliberate practice and a little discipline, you can be or do just about anything! *Little Hinges Swing Big Doors.*

Thoughts and Tools

- Correct practice makes better
- You can improve or even master any skill or ability
- Coaching helps
- Consistency-sustainability are important

Chapter

10

Willpower

I am so lazy, and the thing ahead is so very difficult.

~ John Steinbeck

You can't have a discussion about habits without talking
about willpower—an overrated, not-so-super power. If you
are like me and most other people, we all think we have a lot
of willpower after a couple of cocktails on New Year's Day.
Did you know that statically, January is the biggest month
for new health club memberships, and by the first week in
February, most people have forgotten the address of their
health club? That is why micro habits, environment, and
systems are so crucial.

Willpower is limited. That is why we need to develop
skills, routines, habits, and tricks that keep us from
sabotaging our goals. That is where a mentor, coach, goal
buddy, accountability partner, your associations, and the

environment are crucial. Back to that old saying, "If you hang out with turkeys, you can't soar with the eagles."

Okay, let me ask these questions, and I want you to really, really, think about them and answer honestly:

1. If I were more disciplined, how would my life change?
2. What would I do more of?
3. What would I do less of?
4. What would I want to accomplish over my lifetime?

Please answer those questions on index cards, your phone, computer, Post-it notes, or little signs. Keep them with you for a week, a month, or forever. Keep them where you will see them every day. That's making the invisible visible.

A big reason for developing micro habits is willpower or lack of willpower. Most of us have tried to gut it out, cowboy up, or push through using pure willpower to achieve something. And what we seem to know or should know by now is that it rarely works.

There is much discussion about our ability to improve or not improve willpower. A good resource is Stanford University Professor Kelly McGonigal's book *The Willpower Instinct: How Self-Control Works, Why it Matters, and What Can You Do to Get More Of It.* Here are a few points from her book that will help you develop willpower.

Enemies of Willpower

- Lack of sleep
- Stress, which can cause us to disconnect, forget long term goals, and act out
- Alcohol. It shuts off willpower and lowers inhibitions (I bet you knew this one)

161

- Guilt. Can lower your willpower, make you feel bad or guilty, drain your brainpower
- Beating yourself up

Things that help you build willpower. The prefrontal cortex, your willpower zone, needs energy; it is like a muscle and needs to be exercised, needs rest and nutrition. These things can help:

1. Improved sleep
2. Meditation
3. Exercise
4. Low glycine or plant-based diet
5. Practice (do something small to exercise willpower, start the process)

Everything one reads about self-improvement has a common thread—exercise! From lowering blood pressure, and reducing body fat to improving sleep, your brain, your mood, or willpower, exercise is always on the list. Just saying. Maybe we all need to take the hint. Now, before you start envisioning tortuous gym workouts, exercise comes in many forms. So, it's what floats *your* boat, not mine or someone else's. Some options include:

- Walking
- Running
- Dancing
- Aerobics
- Golf (walk rather than take a cart)
- Tennis, pickle-ball
- Weightlifting (should be part of your regimen for life)
- Martial arts
- (No, crocheting doesn't count unless you are using an exercise bike.)

- Plan on moderate exercise at least 140 minutes per week.

Willpower, rewards, and why we quit. Anytime you do something hard, a certain amount of norepinephrine pushes into your system. Norepinephrine is released and tells us to stop. It's our stop sign, and dopamine is our *go* sign. The good news is dopamine can help us push through the pain and override norepinephrine, hence the need for tiny wins. As the tiny wins mount, the further we go; each win helps us get to the next milestone. The more tiny wins you can create, the more you will be motivated to move forward.

Developing the internal rewards that create dopamine is what helps us create habits. They trigger a stronger need to perform and create a memory to do it again later. So, small internal rewards give us little hits of dopamine to keep us going. It is very important to understand this works both ways, for good or bad habits and behaviors.

Thoughts and Tools

Short chapter about a huge subject that's why I recommend buying and making the time to read Professor Kelly McGonigal's book *The Willpower Instinct, how self-control works, why it matters, and what you can do to get more of it.*

Also, look up Professor Andrew Huberman from the Huberman Lab at Stanford. He has great information, on YouTube & his podcast, that will help you develop willpower, achieve goals, and become healthier.

Remember

- Get more sleep
- Exercise

Willpower

- Pay attention to your diet
- Do small things to increase your willpower

The next chapter will help you develop your willpower by using your environment.

Chapter

11

Environment

"Many people use their environment as a scapegoat for their shortcomings, usually in the form of a complaint: *If it weren't for where I live, I could do something with my life.* If you are not happy with your environment, then change it; you have the ability to do this. If you spend as much energy on seeking solutions as you did on procrastinating, your problems will vanish, and your world would be alive instead of slumbering or dead."

~ Geoff Thompson, author, playwright, and martial arts instructor

"If you do not create and control your environment, your environment will create and control you."
~ Marshall Goldsmith

Environment Plays a Major Factor in Your Success

Have I mentioned your *environment* enough yet? Often-overlooked part of setting up any goal, habit, or system is your environment. I don't believe many people give much thought to the subtleties that contribute to our habits, life, successes, or failures. When I say environment, I mean everything: your home, your room, your office or place of work, your car, and the people. All are crucial. Your environment is made up of people, places, things, sounds, and visuals—things that can propel you forward or distract you and keep you stuck. Distraction is dis-action!

Right now, I'm sitting in the coffee shop, basically alone, at 7:00 a.m. with a cup of hot coffee, working on the next to last chapter. It's an environment that signals my brain that it's time to get to work. I purposely bring only my iPad and a pad of paper.

There are few distractions; the only possible one is a self- distraction of going online, chatting with someone, or daydreaming. Morning is my best time, my willpower is usually strong enough to keep me from distractions. By contrast, at 6:00 p.m., I have less energy and less willpower. It also helps that there are no time vampires lurking in the area.

Distractions are one of our biggest nemeses. We are drunk on our distractions, and it's getting so much easier to be distracted. As the new old saying goes, "Are you using your devices, or are your devices using you?"

Distraction and short attention spans are becoming increasingly significant in our lives. It's so easy to avoid the things we need to do to move forward. Eliminating as many distractions as possible is important—for example, keeping your workspace free of anything that will distract you. Even if you simply put stuff behind you in a box where you can't see it, that helps. Clean your work area. I know how painful this is. I struggle with it all the time. Again, this is why clarity of goals and a system are important. I'm sure you can find many ideas about how to reduce distractions. It's worth your time to take the time to do this and remember every little thing you do helps. Don't let your distractions derail you.

Multi-tasking can cause problems, too. In his excellent book, Thinking Fast and Slow, Daniel Kahneman says, "Switching from one task to another is effortful, especially under time pressure. The need for rapid switching is one of the reasons that advanced mental manipulation is so difficult." That is why multi-tasking doesn't really work; it slows us down and distracts us.

Bob's Second Office

My friend Bob used to have a separate office two miles from his main office. I used to think it was crazy. It was a ten-by-ten-foot room with a desk chair, no phone, no fax—just him and his computer or whatever he was working on at the time. He told me on numerous occasions that he got more done, and some of his best work occurred there. He simply blocked out an appointment on his calendar, and no one knew where he was; he was unreachable. He developed the skill of controlling his environment and becoming a great blockhead (blocking out specific times). Being a blockhead will help you with removing distractions.

Don't be afraid to try something different. Any time we do something new, it takes getting used to it. Patience and persistence are important. It doesn't have to be a private office, it can be the library, a coffee shop, sitting outside by a stream, or anything that will help you eliminate distractions. It is about what works for you. The objective is to get things done—not just doing things the same old way. If you try it, make sure you don't clutter the new location with stuff. Keep it simple. You will find that you don't have to block a lot of time because you will be super productive.

In my book, Find A Way, A Guide to Getting the Most Out of Life, I talk about my friends Bob and Roy and how meeting up with them accidentally at a coffee shop opened my eyes and changed my beliefs about many things. They showed me that I could decide to do something and just do it. They decided to leave their sales jobs at a large life insurance company and start their own businesses in insurance, real estate, and building construction. Yes, they just decided, and they made it happen. My being in their environment changed the way I thought about what was possible. That is what launched my career in business. If I hadn't run into them that day, I do not know what I would be doing. Your environment and the people in it can play a major role in every part of your life. It can change the way you think, act, and develop habits.

Structure and environment are crucial; structure determines behavior. You have a hundred percent control of your environment. Craft your environment so when it's time to function, everything is where it is supposed to be. That way, you are not distracted from your tasks or your goal.

Always remember the rule. "Be selfish with your time and kind to people."

Reduce Drag

Drag can literally drag you down. Distractions are a drag in your environment. Have you ever watched race cars, bicyclists, or tractor-trailer trucks going at higher speeds following each other closely? This is referred to as drafting, and it significantly reduces the effects of drag. Drag is a force, friction, created by air as an object moves forward, and it works against the object. Just like in racing, we need to reduce drag when we are creating good habits. That means removing anything that gets in the way or slows down our progress. It also means that we want to increase drag when we are trying to eliminate habits that don't serve us, bad habits.

Make habits easier to maintain by structuring your environment accordingly. No doubt you've heard of these structures: put your running shoes by the door to make it easier to run; put the cookies in the basement or leave them in your car, so it's inconvenient to get them. This forces you to think, act, and be deliberate. This is "Drag." You need to reduce drag in your environment to promote good habits.

You also need to increase drag for bad habits, making them harder to do. How can you increase drag? If you simply left cookies in the cupboard, it is too easy to get some. If you leave the cookies in the car, you will be less tempted to have some.

Make things that you need to do easy and convenient—that's reducing drag. Here's a recent revelation. I would mentally admonish the store for charging $6.99 for a container of pre-cut strawberries, raspberries, blackberries, or other items. How could they? Yet, I had no problem paying $10 for a grinder at the pizza shop. Then one day, it came to me. This is moronic. You grumble about healthy food that costs $6.99, yet you willingly spend $10 for something that isn't as healthy for you. Now I get it. Buying anything that makes life better and easier reduces drag.

Make it Easier: Reduce Drag

In reducing drag, always remember Parkinson's Law, "The work (task) expands to the time allotted." The longer you give yourself to do something, the longer it will take to get it done.

Environment

Reduce Drag	Increase Drag
Make as much as possible as easy as possible	Put cookies outside or far away
Buy pre-cut fruits and veggies	Make a healthy shopping list (stick to it)
Create strong nudges	Buy healthier snacks
Set reminders for your goals	Turn off the cell phone
Place exercise equipment in a prominent spot	Clean your environment
Make space, specific times, and places to get things done	Turn off social media
Make it fun	Make negative things harder to do
Get a partner	Clean and declutter your environment
Have a workspace way from your normal space	Have specific time limits for social media
Get up and go back to work	

Where to start, change, or reduce drag? I believe for all of us, our number one long-range goal needs to be health. You can always work a little extra and earn a little more money. You can always do a lot of other things if you're healthy; if you're not, it sucks. Create an environment that is conducive to getting healthier and thus getting more of what you want. One of my friends, a fitness coach, uses as a tagline "health is wealth." So true.

How subtle are the effects of our environment on our goals, and our systems? Extremely! Think about this, any time you have a small change in something, a routine, a location, or the people you associate with, it affects your habits. Moving farther away from the gym, work, home, or going off your normal route can cause you to start, change, or ruin a good habit. Moving to a location where it is more convenient to get to the gym, walking paths, or other healthy opportunities reduces drag.

The principle of reducing or increasing drag applies to everything in your environment, making some behaviors you want easier and others not so much. It works for your associations, too—the individuals in your environment who you hang around with. Your GANG plays a big role in scripting your life. If the people in your environment are dragging you down, do your best to change them. The big thing is for you to take charge and realize how all these things interplay. It's important for you to create the environment you need. It's not about anybody else; it's about what you need.

Now, saying that, I realize that you cannot just cut everyone out of your life and replace them. It is about you controlling the time spent with who, doing what, and where. The bottom line is that everything counts, so take control of your environment. The more you learn, listen, and pay attention, the more likely you are to move in the right direction. The direction needs to be the right one for you. Take your environment seriously. Take micro-steps and tread lightly in the beginning.

One thing I want you to remember, everyone is different, so take what you need and use it and modify it to fit you. Here is a caveat. Some people will think this is selfish or mean. I don't think so at all. I think when we improve, we help those around us improve too.

A last word on your environment, distraction, and focus; in Daniel Kahneman's book *Thinking Fast and Slow*, he

Environment

states that your brain *cannot* do two things at the same time. This is the whole multitasking thing. Here is a classic example. You are driving in an unfamiliar area in heavy traffic, and you're trying to think about where you're going. Your radio is blasting loud music, and you say to someone, "Please turn the radio off or down. I can't think?" The reason is that your brain can't focus on what it needs to do. Your brain can jump back and forth very quickly between subjects, but it is an inefficient way to work. This is important, especially when you're in a tight situation where your full attention is required. Don't try to fool yourself into thinking you can do many things at one time. You can't. It's just self-deception. Controlling your environment is crucial to forming new habits and becoming a success.

"We are kept from our goal, not by obstacles,
but by a clear path to lesser goals."
~Robert Brault

Thoughts and Tools

- Reduce drag for good new habits
- Increase drag for habits that don't serve you
- Start small

More on this in the next chapter on Micro habits.

12

Micro Habits

"The goal is not to be perfect by the end. The goal is to be
better tomorrow."
~Simon Sinek

Our habits are the cornerstone of much of our lives. Some
habits serve us well and move us forward; others can stop us
and even kill us. Researchers point out that about 45% of
what we do every day is habitual, and that makes habits
important. From brushing our teeth, showering, dressing to
eating, much is on autopilot both personally and at work.
Paying attention to your habits is paying attention to the
quality of your life.

"When you improve a little each day, eventually big things
occur. When you improve conditioning a little each day,
eventually, you have a big improvement in conditioning.

Environment

> Not tomorrow, not the next day, but eventually, a big gain is made. Don't look for big, quick improvement. Seek small improvements one day at a time. That's the only way it happens—and when it happens, it lasts."
> ~ John Wooden

Read Coach Wooden's quotation again and really take it in. It is the essence of micro habits. Teaching the philosophy of small changes and improvements earned Wooden the stature of being one of the most effective coaches in the history of college basketball.

I first became interested in the concept of micro habits many years ago when I read *One Small Step Can Change Your Life: The Kaizen Way* by Dr. Robert Maurer. He was a member of the UCLA School of Medicine. He was interested in helping people make changes in their lives. I'll give you a few suggestions that will help you. If you want to dive deeper into the available books on creating habits, I'll have a list at the end of this chapter.

Micro Habits

Micro habits are a method for positive change. All too frequently, I see in myself and others the need to change. Yet most often, little happens. I think mostly because we have, for a long time, been bombarded by self-help and motivational gurus and their philosophies, which don't work for the vast majority of people. In fact, I think they scare more people away than they encourage. No doubt, you have heard the slogans:

- Go big or go home
- BHAGs Big Hairy Audacious Goals
- Just do it
- Burn the ships

- All or nothing

Often, the *all-or-nothing* approach leaves us with nothing. I love these adages because they conjure up images of a highly charged "just do it" kind of person who is making things happen. On the other hand, I must admit that sometimes these phrases stop me cold. I know the value of giving it your all. I can intellectualize the idea of pushing through my fears and letting go of my aversion to risk and going for it. However, I also have a keen sense of my tolerance for a "burn the ships" mentality. I know how long the pump of "go big or go home" actually lasts. I think for most people, it lasts until they leave the seminar, turn off YouTube, he video or podcast, put down the book, or within a couple of hours of the pep talk. If that weren't true, many, many more people would be living large or larger. That is why the concept of micro habits intrigues me. I am not saying don't have big aspirations or dreams, a big vision. No, just work on a micro habit plan—a sustainable system to get there.

How much of what you do is habitual? Many neurobiologists, cognitive psychologists, and others -ave suggested that from 45 up to 60% or more of our human behavior is habit. You will have to observe and judge here. I am leaning toward the 45 to 60% range. In other words, a large part of how you think, what you say, and your overall actions, fall into the habit category.

Habits are involuntary behaviors, and actions are controlled and hardwired deep in your subconscious mind. Your subconscious learns slowly by repetition, and once it learns, it becomes automatic. That is why once you create a habit, trying to change it can take a long time.

Think about all the things you do automatically now that at one time may have required a lot of conscious effort. Things like reading this book, writing, skiing, riding a bike, driving a car, walking, operating a computer, talking—all were at one time difficult. Now, you do them without thinking. That's great for habits that help you, not so great for ones that don't. Bad habits can overrule goals, which is why we often say one thing and do another. Paying attention to your habits is extremely important for attaining your goals and improving your life.

Why Micro Habits?

Micro means small, and micro habits are small yet powerful. Think about microtechnology in medicine. Scientists hope to inject a person with microscopic nanobots that will go directly to the source of disease and repair or deliver medicine without damaging the body. Micro habits will do the same for your life, career, business, relationships, or finances. Micro changes, if done well and long enough, can lead to explosive success.

Let's look at the reality. Most of us never accomplish all our aspirations. Most of us leave this planet with far too much-unused potential. A few people may accomplish some or a lot, but that's rare. Part of the reason we are often afraid of success is "What Other People Think." One goal of micro habits is not scaring yourself or those around you.

Any time you have a big ambition, especially if it is right in front of you, it's very easy to scare the crap out of yourself and talk yourself out of it before you start. That is why taking small steps and improving over a longer period of time is a great way to build confidence, skills, and success. As Professor Jordan Peterson says, "You need to be willing to start by doing something badly." Then, you can improve and do it well.

Taking small steps toward a large goal is helpful for many people, especially when they involve things that are not fun or if they have lots of other things going on, which most of us do. And as I like to say, once the initial spark or excitement wears off from anything, we enter "The Valley of

Dead **Dreams**." Micro habits can help us avoid or get across the valley.

When we think about something that our brain assumes could be dangerous, challenging, or energy-consuming, it looks for ways to stop us from taking action. Your brain likes the status quo; it hates using energy, and it hates change. Yup, your brain is lazy. That's why it creates habits—to save thinking and energy. Anything new or perceived as challenging sets off our brain's alarm system—our fight, flight, or freeze reaction. So, when you decide on something big, your alarm system goes on alert: Code red: Ding-ding! Danger! Put on the brakes! You might get hurt, fail, or look stupid. This is too much work or the infamous WOPT. One of the goals of micro habits is to avoid setting off the alarm, to fly under the radar, tiptoe past your brain's warning and protection systems.

Now, it doesn't always work; there are occasions when we need to push through and step up to the plate to hit a home run now—for example, tackling that report or presentation that is due tomorrow or the sales calls that must be made today. However, had you started by taking small steps on that report or presentation two weeks ago, you would be in better shape. Remember, too, from Chapter One, when those situations present themselves, just start and let a body in motion work for you.

"It does not matter how slowly you go as long as you don't stop."
~ Confucius

My 2-5-15 Rule, Micro Steps at Work that can Grow and Make it Easy!

Here is something I often do, and it can help. If you want to exercise, start small. Make something so small that you can't find enough excuses not to do it. A good example is to start by walking 500 steps a day. Never discount the power of a small start. All too often, we want to do something, and then what happens? The excuses start. "I don't have time to work." "What's the use in trying? I always quit anyway." We get into all-or-nothing thinking. If you get into all-or-nothing thinking, guess what? You get nothing! As my friend, Charlie Cook, famous for his *Gun Grams* and *Riding Shotgun with Charlie* Vlog, likes to say, "Stop using excuses like there is a reward."

That is why making any new thing like a habit *easy* is important. Keeping it short, sweet, simple, and sustainable gets rid of many of your excuses. Thus, my 2-5-15 rule. You only have to do something for 2 minutes; that's it. There are things you can get done in 2 minutes, 5 minutes, 15 minutes, or at least things you can start. I often find when I start working on something, even for 2 minutes, I might do 5, 10, 15, or even 20 minutes. Always remember that you only need to do 2 minutes to help you start creating a new habit. So, if I'm going to exercise for 2 minutes every day, how many excuses can I make? Really, it's only 2 minutes. Again, often 2 minutes turns into 5, 10, or 20. The key is you are establishing a habit. You are becoming someone who exercises, writes, and so forth.

This is an important time so *pay attention* because here is where your mind goes to work, and it starts questioning. "Oh, this is a bunch of crap. Two minutes. Is he kidding? This is stupid. It won't work. This guy is a crackpot." My answer? What do you have to lose? Two minutes! The easier a behavior is, the more likely you are to repeat it!

"The goal is not to be perfect by the end. The goal is to be better tomorrow."
~Simon Sinek

Here is a true-life example. Three years ago, I started doing squats every morning. Not my favorite exercise. Sometimes I used weights, sometimes not. I started by doing 10 per day. It may sound silly, but that's what I did because I couldn't come up with enough excuses not to do 10. It was easy. Then after a week, I went to 12, then 15, then two sets of 12. Now I do a minimum of 100 to 120 every morning before showering. I haven't missed a day in three years. That translates to 90,000 to 100,000 squats! And there have been challenge weeks when I've done 1,000 for the week. If we make things too big or too hard, we continually skip them, give up, or never start, and we never develop the habit.

Yes, there is that rare person who starts huge and keeps going. And you and I both know it's rare. But as I said earlier, it's about sustainability. It's about Keep It Simple, Sustainable, Easy, and Supported. Keep it so simple it's impossible to fail. And if you should fall off track, it is easy to get back on. Here is another good practice to develop: never miss two days in a row. A big part of the process is getting back on track.

This is what micro habits are all about. They are about building *sustainable* and continuous improvement by doing small things over time. If you can master this, it will truly change your life.

There are all kinds of small things you can do. Let's suppose you have a garden, and you have a problem with weeds. Every time you walk in your garden, pull 10 weeds. "Oh, that's it?" you may say. Yes, that's it. I am not kidding. If you walk through the garden twice a day, you've pulled 20 weeds. In the course of a week, 140 weeds are gone. You see, when we make things all or nothing, the usual choice for most people is nothing. One other tip. I leave my weeding tool in the garden where I can't miss it and don't waste time looking for it. Bingo! Another habit that's easily sustained.

You may not be able to use micro habits in everything you do, but you can certainly use them in many areas. They will add up and make a big difference. Here are a couple more examples. Suppose you want to save money, but you've been saving none. While saving even one dollar a day can seem silly, in a year, that's $365, which is still better than zero. Over ten-plus years, a modest return of six percent is $4,810; in twenty years, that's $13,426. Now imagine if you worked your way up to $2, $3, or $5.

You could work one or two extra hours per week if you have a job that allows for that. If not, find something part-time on the side; save or invest that extra money. With time and patience, the results will be awesome.

Micro habits can even help in your relationships. Saying one or more nice things to your spouse, partner, friend, mom, dad, customer, employee, or boss will make a big difference.

Whether pulling weeds, exercising, saving money, or big and small tasks, micro habits work. The key is to develop those that are easy to start and easy to sustain. Sustainability and a little discipline are the keys to your success in every area of life.

What comes first is developing micro habits?

To start any habit, you must want to accomplish something. You want to lose weight, start a garden, exercise, make more cold calls, have a better relationship, get better grades, write a book, or save more money. Next, you need to commit to a process, one that supports your desire and is *easy* to start, do, and sustain. For the majority of us, desire, commitment, and willpower won't do it. It's limited. You need to commit to a process, one that supports your desire and is easy to do.

Micro Habit Process

What are the elements required to develop a micro habit? Let's start with:

1. The Nudge
2. Motivation (Desire, commitment)
3. Ability to do it, capacity (and reducing drag?)
4. Rewards, internal & external

Nudge means to touch or push gently to get a person's attention. Nudges are reminders. They may be physical, auditory, visual, people, places, or times. Why is nudge the first component of forming a habit? While you need to want to do something and have the ability to do it, the key is having a system! And that starts with a nudge, a reminder, or a push.

A nudge is the time or place preceding a new behavior—a gentle push. We all need motivation, yet how often have you said, "I am motivated," and not much happens? Why? Because you need a clear, easy system to create a micro habit. A clear system means what, when, where, and how. A nudge is tying a micro habit to something you already do automatically every day: brushing your teeth, eating lunch, bedtime, getting up, or and coming home. Each of these is a

Environment

potential nudge you can link the new behavior to, either just before or right after. Your nudge is your prompt or reminder to your brain, "Oh, it's time to__(insert goal)."

Examples of Common Nudges

Brushing teeth	Phone reminders
Getting up	Going to bed
Before or after meals	Making coffee or tea
Getting dressed or undressed	Making your bed
Before work	Turning on a computer
After work	Break time at work
Picking up the remote	Taking a shower
Putting the kids to bed	Using the bathroom

Motivation

In addition to nudge, there are other elements in creating new habits: desire, want, aka motivation. You have to want to do something or accomplish something. That is the ignition switch, the commitment: no want, no motivation, no need to take action. A vital component of your motivation to do something is *clarity*. Exactly what do you want? How does that look? When do you want it?

Here's a good example I learned years ago, and I've used it with people in my seminars. Someone will say, "I want more money."

So I hand them a dollar bill and say, "Now you have more money. Now what?"

The response I usually get is, "I wanted more than that."

I reply, "Well, how would anyone know if you are not clear? How do you know yourself?"

The key is to be clear about how much money you want, just like for any other goal. Exactly what do you want and by when? Then you can build a system of habits to get you there. Without a specific amount and timeframe, how do you know what to do? Once you have the information and it is crystal clear, you can work backward and develop a plan to get what you want. For example, how much do I need to save each day, week, month, or year? How do I invest that money to my advantage to get to my goal? Do I need help with this? Who could help me with this? What will be my nudges? Clarity of the goal brings clarity to the process and motivation.

The same would apply to how many new clients you may want for your business, how fast you want to pay off your mortgage, how healthy you want to be, or how much you want to weigh. Anything basically can be fit into a time frame. If you do not have clarity, most likely, you will struggle. Be clear about what you want!

Next comes ability. You have to have the ability to achieve the goal or behavior. Or you must be able to develop the ability. This is the capacity to do something, create something for yourself.

Let's say you want to play the drums. You can buy a drum kit, take lessons, watch videos, and practice; you have the ability. An example of non-ability, as in my case, let's say I want to be a top-notch singer. I would need at least some natural ability, which I have none. So could I learn to sing a few tunes? Yes, but that is where it would end. No matter how much time, coaching, or practice, trust me, there would be limited success. That is why, for whatever it is you want to accomplish, there must be at least some chance of success, also known as being practical. Motivation, wanting, commitment, and all those things are wonderful as long as you mix them with at least some practicality. Also, your environment must be conducive to success as well as reducing or creating drag as much as possible depending on the desired behavior.

During the process, here are three simple steps to help change the habit process:

1. Make it easy
2. Make it fit you
3. Make it rewarding

Rewards

Make establishing a new habit as much fun as possible. Fun is often in the mind; make it a challenge, challenge yourself to do better, and keep challenging yourself. You will be surprised how mentally rewarding it is.

Most of our rewards need to be internal recognition of our micro accomplishments. You can also use a few external rewards like a walk, five minutes surfing the net, listening to music, taking a drive, or watching your favorite show. Rewards should be positive and not counterproductive. In other words, don't work out and then have a huge ice cream sundae. Everything needs to fit into place and be aligned with your program, goal, wants, and micro habits.

Many things here may sound too good to be true or too small to make a difference. Finding ways to make changes or accomplishing goals easier is what life is about. My mentor, Tolly Burkan, an internationally known seminar presenter and author, says, "If you are riding a horse, sit in the saddle in the direction the horse is going. Don't make it harder." Whenever possible, remove or reduce temptation because we do not want to "get caught up in the thick of thin things, things that take time but mean little in moving you in the direction you want to go." Control people, places, and things in your life that stop or hinder you. After all, it is your life.

Keys

The key to setting up good habits is structure—your system. Your system means a process that works for you. Three components of these habits are when you do them, how long they take, and where you do them.

Several university psychology researchers have found that having a specific time, duration, and place increases your ability to create new and better habits. It's a system. And as I said before, it's also freedom. Mental freedom because the work, goal, or task is done, and it is not hanging over or nagging you.

Another factor in creating habits is knowing your personality style. In short, know yourself. It always goes back to "Who I am and how I operate." What works and what does not work for you and then building your system around you. If you haven't done it, I suggest you take the Myers-Briggs Type Indicator—a quick and easy set of questions that may give you some insight. There is also the Strengths Finder 2.0 at www.gallup.com. I would do both. They are among a plethora of resources that will help you. As Aristotle said, "Knowing yourself is the beginning of wisdom."

Exercise seems to be a universal issue. Let's say you are introverted and do not always want to be around a lot of people, so going to the gym is out, or you could go off-peak or explore other options, like running or walking. A home gym may work best. If you are extroverted, the opposite may work better for you. Pay attention and know yourself. Very few people seem to be able to gut it through in the long run, so making it easier makes it better.

Environment

Nature

Always remember that we are human, and we have millions of years of being human and only a hundred or so years of really being modern . . . if that. So, we're always going to be up against our internal survival instincts. Survival means eating, being in a tribe, and protection—those things haven't changed even though our environment has. That means for survival, we want to consume food, and our brain wants us to conserve energy by being lazy and doing nothing dangerous or fearful. It is our job to recognize all those factors and use that knowledge to move forward, to get better—not perfect, but better.

It is important to pay attention to human behavior, to your behavior, understanding that we hold beliefs that may be counterproductive to our wants. It's a funny thing -- your brain wants to keep you safe and save energy, yet it provides you with imagination and an amazing amount of potential you can never reach if you don't take risks and use your energy.

Create micro habits by starting with small questions:

- What small, easy thing could I do to improve my health?
- What could I do for two minutes that would help my health?
- What could I avoid doing for two minutes that would enhance my health?

Take small actions. Identify five small actions to improve your health:

- Exercise two minutes every
- Drink one extra glass of water
- Go to bed two minutes earlier and get up two minutes earlier

- Eat one-fourth less of one piece of toast
- Cut out a pinch of sugar from your coffee (additional pinch every 2-3 weeks)

There Are No Guarantees

There are no guarantees in life except one: if you don't continually grow and improve, you go backward, and your life will not be anywhere near as rewarding as it could be. That means we don't stop—we just keep moving forward. We don't slow down just because there's no guarantee. We keep adjusting, adapting, improving, and moving forward. As Rocky Balboa would say, "That's how winning is done." I often say, "Do what you love, or love what you do." You can develop a passion for almost anything. The blind notion of simply following your passion has led many people down a path of failure, financial ruin, and frustration. Maybe a better word would be to follow a practical passion. Find something you like, then make a living at it. Otherwise, you're setting yourself up for misery.

There's always time to do your passion on the side. I run several businesses, and I have a passion for personal development and writing short articles and iBooks as well, but that's not my livelihood. My livelihood gives me time to do those other things and gives me funds to do those things. I'm able to self-publish a book, and even if it doesn't sell one copy, it won't hurt me financially. Many years ago, a very famous and successful restaurateur in my town said to me, "Dennis, if you're going to be in business, make sure that whatever you do or sell, people have to have it. That way, you'll be recession-proof." He said, "This is why I don't sell fancy food; when things get bad, people don't go to the fancy restaurants, but they'll still come here." Good advice from a man who started with an ice cream stand and developed what

Environment

was at the time, the 35th largest single location grossing restaurant in the United States of America.

Tools and Thoughts

- We are meant to learn and grow until the end
- It is a trial-and-error process or trial-and-success process
- KISSES-Keep It Simple, Sustainable, Easy, and Supported
- Never miss twice
- Your environment is crucial
- Be clear: what, when, where, and how long
- Two minutes can be a good start
- Good habits - read every day
- Reduce drag when creating positive habits
- Increase drag when working on eliminating bad habits
- Small rewards
- Remove distractions as much as possible
- Don't set yourself up for failure by thinking you are superhuman
- Be selfish with your time and kind to people

"You are more likely to act yourself into feeling than feel yourself into action."
~Jerome Bruner Harvard University

Most of us can do far more than we let ourselves do. You can have almost anything you want if you are willing to give your time, money, energy and give up your doubts and fears.

This is not the end of the book; it is the beginning of you.

The Beginning

About the Author

From a minimum wage job to a millionaire in 12 years. Quitting college to become a self-employed businessman at age 23. Dennis understands what it takes to be successful. His company, the McCurdy Group, was awarded the prestigious five-star designation in 2003. Dennis has started ten businesses and has bought, owned, sold, and rehabbed millions of dollars in real estate.

Dennis speaks frequently about personal development and growth, in his 5-week Workshop "Find A Way" which was developed for individuals who want to invigorate their life, reach for their dreams, and learn new ways to achieve. Those who have attended his presentations agree that Dennis is a practical and down-to-earth coach/guide. No Frills, just lots of meat and potatoes.

Dennis is also the author of Find A Way, A Guide to Getting The Most Out of Life, 52 Ways to Find A Way, and "Suck It Up, Cupcake, Stop Screwing Yourself and Get the Life You Want." Having grown up in a small rural New England town with no role models for success, Dennis sucked it up and found a way. Dennis speaks about success from the point of view of an average person; he walks the talk. Dennis is a United States Air Force veteran.

www.ingramcontent.com/pod-product-compliance
Lightning Source LLC
Chambersburg PA
CBHW072346090426
42741CB00012B/2940